THE ROCK CRIES OUT

DISCOVERING ETERNAL TRUTH
IN UNLIKELY MUSIC

STEVE **STOCKMAN**

Published by Relevant Books

A division of Relevant Media Group, Inc.

www.relevantbooks.com

www.relevantmediagroup.com

Design: Relevant Solutions

www.relevant-solutions.com

Interior design by Matt Crow

For information or bulk orders, contact:

RELEVANT MEDIA GROUP, INC.

POST OFFICE BOX 951127

LAKE MARY, FL 32795

407-333-7152

Library of Congress Control Number: 2003096210

International Standard Book Number: 0-9729276-5-4

04 05 06 07 9 8 7 6 5 4 3 2 1

Printed in the United States of America

To my wife Janice and my daughters Caitlin and Jasmine who had to endure (or enjoy) so much time without a husband and father when I was researching and writing this book.
I love you so much!

"let us head up north again ... "

Thank yous to all of the following who gave me clues and hints and books and encouragement: Tim Flaherty, Geoff Bailie, Gordon Ashbridge, Chris Fry, Rosie Cowan, Paul Chambers, Martyn Joseph, Dave Magee, Gareth Higgins, Alain Emerson, Steffan McNally, David Dark, Sarah Dark, Mark Houston, Brian Houston, Pete Rawlins, David Smith, Ken Heffner, Paul Bowman, Alister Topping, Paul Zahl, Gil Kracke, Stewart Dickson, Dennis Hollinger, Gar Saegar, Oliver Carruthers, Jude Adam, William Crawley, Colin Cameron, Clare Orr, Habitat for Humanity NI, Grant Edkins, Donné Jones, Vido, Nosuko at Habitat For Humanity Cape Town, Spiwo Xapile, Ace and ZL Zwane Memorial Church, Guguletu, Hectors House, Greenbelt, Summer Madness, *Paste* magazine, Third Way, *Phantom Tollbooth*, BBC Radio Ulster, IFES Ireland, and students of the Presbyterian Chaplaincy at Queens University Belfast—particularly those who live with me at Derryvolgie Hall for allowing me to unravel my thoughts publicly!

Thanks to all at Relevant Books for patience and courage.

Love to Sam and Margaret Stockman and Bryan and Anne Gordon, Lynn Ferguson, Gareth and Lorna Dunlop, Carole McMahon, Cary Pate, Dave, Olwyn, and Luke and Lily Adams, Rob, Ro, Aoife and Bethan O'Farrell-Lawson, Tim, Sarah, Emily, and Matthew Wray, Iris Ashbridge, Chris Guiney.

More love than I can ever give to Janice, Caitlin, and Jasmine who give more love and joy than I can ever deserve.

INTRODUCTION

This book began on the radio. Not like Garrison Keilor's Woebegone Days (I wish!). In 1996 BBC Radio Ulster asked me to take the chair of their religious contemporary music program, *The Gospel Show*. As the History of BBC Northern Ireland put it, "Steve Stockman was given total freedom on his Sunday night music show." I often wonder if I have abused the freedom, but I am still in the chair seven years on, so that must say something.

I started out by playing mainly what I saw as the best of what was happening in contemporary Christian music as my predecessor had done, although I moved it away from Michael Card and Michael W. Smith and toward Delirious?, The Newsboys, dcTalk, Larry Norman, Charlie Peacock, and Sarah Masen. Then I got more courageous and started to add artists who were Christians but do not do their "thang" in the

Christian subculture, adding the likes of U2, Bruce Cockburn, Victoria Williams, and The Vigilantes of Love. This gave the show a little more depth and bite and opened many listeners up to new music that would get lost between mainstream playlistings and my very specialized one. Most of them seemed to have heard of U2 though!

Eventually, I started to play artists with no Christian commitment at all. I think the first such artist might have been David Gray, whose song, "Let The Truth Sting," seemed too appropriate and powerful to ignore. Radiohead, Tom Waits, Jackson Browne, and all of the artists who are featured in this book were soon added to the roster of "secular saints" or even "pagan prophets" and became regular fixtures on the show. I realized very quickly that my audience was a very wide range of ages and tastes. Some wanted to hear the best new music, but there were some who hated the music and wanted some chat. I tried to maintain that balance, almost weaving a sermon around the words of the songs. My reason or excuse to play David Gray, or Radiohead, or whoever, was to give some insight to those who were not sure what was going on in the "real world."

Last year I realized that the Christian music on my show had become a small percentage of what gets played. When I was gazing across the CD shelves on a Sunday afternoon looking for songs that would be what Guthrie called "not just good, but good for something," I regularly discovered that those without a faith had said something more spiritual than those claiming to be making "Christian" music. In the end we had to change the name of the show to *Rhythm and Soul*, as *The Gospel Show* had ceased to be an accurate description.

So this book has been playlisted the same way as my radio show. The artists are chosen because I have been using their work and bringing out spiritual truth from their songs for seven years. I have confined it to artists who have never professed a Christian faith, with the exception of Lauryn Hill, whose faith straddles Christianity and Rastafarianism but whose message in her *MTV Unplugged 2.0* album is too essential to leave out!

These are not biographies. If you are looking for biographies of these artists, there are really good ones out there already, apart from Jackson Browne, who seriously needs one. Biographical detail appears in some essays more than in others. The structure of each essay is different. In some we look at entire careers; Bruce Springsteen's is about the difference in his view of God at the beginning of his career and how it has changed until where it is now. On the other hand, Lauryn Hill is based solely on one performance that became a DVD and CD. The most of Ani DiFranco's is based on one song, and through it we take a long look at September 11. Kurt Cobain's is not even based so much on his work as on his death.

My attitude throughout these essays is that the glass is half full. There may be the occasional criticism of the artist, but that is not the point. There is probably an entirely different book where someone simply interrogates the work and lives of these artists and finds all the things in their lives that collide with the Christian faith. I had no desire to write such a book. For me it was how these artists caressed with my faith. These artists have been friends I have never met, who in my car, my front room, my office, and the radio studio have whispered truth to me from on and between the lines of their magnificent songs.

I hope in my subjective engagement of the work of these twelve great artists there will be helpful, objective truth. The greatest danger in something so subjective is that I would abuse the work of the artists in order to say what I wanted them to say. In my subjectivity, I have tried hard to maintain the integrity of the original work.

The Church and America are on the harsh end of much criticism in this book. Where my political perspective screams through, forgive me, but never dismiss the critique until you are absolutely sure that there is no truth in there that needs to be dealt with. The prophets were always quite scathing of their nation and believing community. It is with harsh truth that God sometimes breaks into our apathy and lethargy. In many ways these artists have said prophetic things that need to be heard and discussed. These are not the definitive answers to the issues in our nation or the Church, but I hope they will add something to the conversation.

There are a few conversations, to which I hope this will contribute. I received a telephone call from a journalist in Florida recently who was researching an article on why a young church had replaced the worship songs in its services with secular music. I shared with him that I sensed that our Christian art was too narrow and not touching many areas of people's spiritual experience. I was involved on the fringes of a more raging conversation in a Christian college where they had started to invite artists without a Christian profession to play on campus. The alumni were up in arms at such a suggestion. What good would it be to have such concerts? Indeed, would it not be detrimental to the spiritual development of the students?

It is a wonderfully refreshing thing that there are fewer books about how demonic the arts are than there were twenty years ago. Writers such as Steve Turner and Bill Romanowski have contributed a more positive approach in cultural criticism than the dualistic tendencies of the recent past, and writers such as Philip Yancey, Ken Gire, and Eugene Peterson among others, have used literature, art, and music references in their writing. This book is a humble contribution, but I hope it is a useful addition to that canon as we seek to understand how followers of Jesus can engage with the modern world, rather than hide away from it.

THE CARESS OF GOD'S GRACE: AM I LOOKING[1]

Am I looking for warmth in the drunkard's eye
Am I looking for the bright in the night time sky
Am I looking down alleys for some kind of epiphany
Am I looking for magic in the everyday ordinary
Am I looking for misunderstanding in an angry fist
Am I looking for the beauty behind the mist
Am I looking in the puddle for the colors incandescent
Am I looking in the mirror for a trace of the transcendent

Am I looking always looking
Eyes open, open wide
Am I looking always looking
At beyond and at the inside

Am I looking for forever in the gembok's dance
Am I looking for some meaning in this lucky chance
Am I looking the trash for some hope of resurrection
Am I looking 'neath the scars for some object of affection
Am I looking for now in the old man's song
Am I looking for the truth where it shouldn't belong
Am I looking in my pride for some reason for confession
Am I looking in my sins for the spirit's helpful lessons

Am I looking always looking
Eyes open, open wide
Am I looking always looking
At beyond and at the inside

Do I see the caress of God's grace
In the kiss blown by a little child
Do I see the caress of God's grace
In the stranger's passing smile
Do I see the caress of God's grace
In a loved one's gentle hand
Do I see the caress of God's grace
In the melody of a rock 'n' roll band

ONE

I
n July and August 2002, my students and I worshiped in JL Zwane Memorial Church on the Guguletu township in Cape Town, South Africa. On the first Sunday we were there, I was asked to say a little bit about my group. We were there to build houses on the townships with Habitat For Humanity, but when I started to explain why we had chosen Cape Town, I was led into a little epiphany. In explaining my rage at apartheid and my following of their story, I suddenly came to realize that it had not been pulpits or Christian conferences or Christian books that had raised my righteous anger against the institutional racism the people in the congregation before me had experienced. Those who had prophesied into my world were for the most part not even of a Christian profession. They were rock musicians.

There was Peter Gabriel's song, "Biko." Stephen Biko was a black leader killed in police custody in 1977 (the book *Cry Freedom*, by white journalist Donald Woods, was later depicted in the film featuring Denzel Washington). There was Little Steve Van Zandt, best known for his work with Bruce Springsteen, who, having been intrigued by Gabriel's song, traveled to South Africa and then came home to write a song that cataloged the main injustices, but proclaimed most particularly that he "ain't gonna play Sun City," South Africa's version of Las Vegas where Western bands were tempted with large offers of money to break the boycott against the white government and play in the country. The song was broken up for a vast array of stars to take different lines, including Bono, Miles Davis, Bonnie Raitt, and a few artists who are featured in this book—Bruce Springsteen, Bob Dylan, and Jackson Browne. The resulting album, which included a Bono solo version of "Silver and Gold," that later would appear on U2's *Rattle and Hum* record and movie, was perhaps the main impetus for a Free Nelson Mandela concert at Wembley Stadium on June 11, 1988. Rock music had sparked my awareness and fanned into flame a rage against such injustices that led me to contribute in the tiniest way to the healing as I worked on these townships where I was now speaking.

Sometimes we find the truth where we have been told it shouldn't belong, eternal truth in the seemingly most unlikely music. On the CD booklet of an album by County Antrim songwriter Bob Speer, I discovered a poem he had printed by Irish poet Patrick Kavanagh that threw some light on such a thought.

> *I saw Christ today*
> *At a street corner stand*
> *In the rags of a beggar he stood*
> *He held ballads in his hand*

He was crying out "Two a penny
Will anyone buy
The finest ballads ever made
From the stuff of joy"

But the blind and deaf went past
Knowing only there
An uncouth ballad seller
With tail-matted hair

And I whom men call fool
His ballads bought
Found him who the pieties
Have vainly sought.[1]

So often we are not looking. So often we are taught not
to look. So often we are convinced that it is wrong to
look. There is a bizarre arrogance that pervades in many
Christian circles that truth is confined to those who have
a seamless profession of faith. The reasoning goes that a
believing psychologist will do a better job than one who
has no faith no matter how much better qualified or gifted
the latter is.

Such thinking is even more acute when it comes to the
arts. I remember when I was serving as assistant minister
in First Antrim Presbyterian Church. I was drawn to the
side by a well meaning, caring, and godly lady who told
me she was concerned for my soul. What had I done? My
brain scanned the previous week to find some action that
might deserve the sack. "Last Wednesday night after the
prayer meeting (and you had prayed so well), I saw you
going into a video shop." Yes! "Well, it isn't a Christian video shop, you know." No, that is why I was in it! It probably
shouldn't have, but it took me aback—not enough though
to prevent a rather mischievous defense. "I was showing
the young people a video. You know, in these postmodern

existentialist days, it is good to watch what perpetrates through the media, particularly Hollywood. We were just trying to discuss the issues." She left confused and no less concerned about my soul.

Christian music and films and novels and everything else have appeared in the market because Christians do not think that it is good to be entertained by "secular" art. As well as the safety angle, there is also, of course, the idea that Christian art will be communicating truth, whereas the "secular" will perpetrate lies. As an example of such a mindset, we need only look at the response Amy Grant or Sixpence None The Richer received from breaking out of the "Christian market" and finding success in the "real world." It was portrayed immediately as a losing of faith, the slippery slope of backsliding into the abyss. As a result we have created a vast industry that, as well as making Christian businessmen bucketloads of money, has also isolated the Christian faith in a ghetto.

So there are Christian pop stars and celebrities, magazines and memorabilia. The extent of the sadness struck me one afternoon as I stood browsing in a Christian bookshop. Over the store PA came some inoffensive worship music, and then suddenly a woman was shouting over the top of "Our God Reigns," "up 2, 3, 4 ... down 2, 3, 4," and I realized that this was Christian aerobics! We cannot even do our exercises to music that isn't Christian!

There is another problem with Christian art. Most of it is evangelistic and thus limited in its ability to communicate the widest of human experiences and the breadth of truth with which the Bible is concerned. If we look at Christian music, we will find that its main focus is either evangelism or worship. There are very few songs on Christian albums about poverty or social justice or racism. A student came to my door recently and asked me what Christian artists

he could listen to who had a political message and a righteous anger. I had to tell him that the Christian industry
would never allow songs on such subjects.

I was thankfully able to guide him to many artists who
have a Christian faith and record and perform outside of
the Christian market for that and other reasons. Artists like
Bruce Cockburn, The Vigilantes of Love, Victoria Williams,
Pedro the Lion, and U2 have given a Christian perspective on a wider range of subject matter that will be of help
to believers as they untangle a spiritual worldview, and
have also been able to, in a much more meaningful way
than the Christian subculture ever will, be involved in the
conversations going on in the wider culture. Yet what a
travesty that many biblical issues are ignored and actively
discouraged when Christian songwriters are plying their
craft.

It is not a healthy thing to limit your reading or listening to
Christian music and books. Listening to the world and the
Word and perceiving where they caress and collide has
been a long held discipline within Christianity. Theologian
Karl Barth spoke about holding the Bible in one hand and
the newspaper in the other. For the purpose of this book,
I have paraphrased "newspaper" with "CD collection."
John Stott would refer to this as "double listening."[2] In his
book, *The Contemporary Christian*, Stott was at pains to
give wisdom as to how to keep Christianity contemporary
and biblical. He asked, "How can we develop a Christian
mind which is both shaped by the truths of historical, biblical Christianity, and acquainted with the realities of the
contemporary world?"[3] He answered in two stages. First:
"We refuse to become either so absorbed in the Word,
that we escape into it and fail to let it confront the world,
or so absorbed in the world, that we conform to it and fail
to subject it to the judgment of the Word."[4] After the re-
fusal, we then come to our double listening. As well as lis-

tening to the Word expectantly, we need to: "listen to the world with critical alertness, anxious to understand it too, and resolved not necessarily to believe and obey it, but to sympathize with it and to seek grace to discover how the gospel relates to it."

When I was going out to preach during my university days, my friend Ian would always say that I should listen to Jackson Browne's *Late For The Sky* album before I left my room. By doing so, I would gain an insight into the mindset of my audience that enabled me to apply the Word of God to the heart of their situation, rather than speak words into the air in some chaotic kind of way.

I would like to hold to this double listening, but then take it another step further. In double listening the Word is more often than not applied to the limitations, flaws, failures, and emptiness of the world. What I am suggesting in this book is that we can learn from the world. I do not mean by that that the world can overrule or speak outside of the Word, my belief is that it can heighten awareness to the truths contained in the Word that should be released into our lives and society.

In his book, *Soul Survivor*, Philip Yancey writes about a number of people who saved his faith when his church experience had damaged and abused his soul. It is a fantastic book of inspirational and mostly unorthodox (in spirit and personality) lives that urge you to suck the marrow out of life. Many would be looked on suspiciously by many regular evangelical Christians, but one would raise most questions. Mahatma Ghandi was not a Christian. Indeed, he rejected Christianity because of what he had seen it do and not do in the world he lived in. Yancey shows that in Ghandi he found a lot more of Christ than he did in Christianity.

So as well as listening to the world, Yancey is suggesting we can learn from the world, that we can find Christ even in those who do not profess Christianity. This does make sense. There are issues that Christians take seriously that sections of the world also take seriously. Christians do not have a monopoly on truth, nor are they the only ones concerned about the issues that Jesus was concerned about. Indeed, it can often seem that people who do not claim a Christian profession are more concerned with kingdom things than the Church.

Clement of Alexandra would have believed philosophy was used to bring the Greeks to Christ the way the law was to the Hebrews. In other words, God had a witness in the non-Jewish world, as well inside that communion, that had a clearer understanding of who He was. Justin Martyr had a similar belief. In another of his books, *The Incomparable Christ*, John Stott wrote, "How is it then that the philosophers came to know the truths they knew? It was partly that (so he claimed) Plato borrowed from Moses and the prophets. But it was also that the divine logos who had been in the world from the beginning and became fully incarnate in Jesus Christ, was distributed by the divine sower everywhere. Thus 'there seem to be seeds of truth among all men.'"[5]

In Athens, Paul found truth in the works of art in the philosophies and love poems of the Greek world. He took them and then used them to bring about a leading toward the ultimate truth about God and the universe.[6] Some more conservative scholars would attempt to suggest that Paul's tactics in Athens were in error and that he repented when in his letter to Corinth he said, "Woe to me if I don't preach the Gospel," but this is hermeneutical gymnastics by those keen to avoid any kind of double listening or cultural engagement.[7] When the Spirit inspired Luke to write it down, he did not inspire him to rebuke Paul's actions at the Areopagus. It was as vital a part of the Spirit's follow-up work to Jesus as any other sermon in the account.

Even though he was not a believer, Cyrus was a Persian king who God appointed to bring His children back from exile and rebuild the temple. I studied Cyrus in the same year that I read Bob Geldof's autobiography, *Is That It?*, while I was in college. As Geldof suggested that God knocked on the door of a scruffy irreverent punk from Dublin who sang about not being interested in charity but only interested in "Looking After Number 1," and asked him to feed the world, I could not help but think he was a Cyrus of his day. God is not confined to those who follow Him to bring about His purposes. I mentioned this in my book *Walk On: The Spiritual Journey of U2*, but it could be that when the Church that claimed to follow Jesus, who said, "Love your neighbor as yourself," were apathetic to the hungry, to embarrass them, God got "the punk rocks" to cry out, but the Church was too lethargic to even blush![8] It was Geldof who caused me to coin a phrase "secular saint," which I use for those artists who do saintly things without any spiritual foundation—not that he was a saint in a theological way at all. It is purely a catch phrase, using poetic licence, to describe those whose music or life is of a spiritual benefit, but who would not claim membership of any Christian (sacred) community.

In the present day, the Church in the West has lost most of its power and influence. Through all kinds of errors of judgment in its interaction with the society, they are marginalized and adrift. Will God let society lose the right questions because the Church has been spewing out irrelevant answers? Or will He continue to keep to the forefront of society those issues that will prevent evil from running amuck and keep us from spiritual anarchy? Jesus told the people that if they did not worship Him, the very rocks would cry out. As well as double listening, we need

to begin to listen for the rocks crying, God at work beyond
the human boundaries we have set for Him.

On a beautiful hot summer's day, I was walking with my
family along the seafront in my beloved Ballycastle on
the north coast of Ireland. As my daughters played on the
climbing frames and slides, I sat down. Gazing out at the
breathtaking coastline, I prayed that I would never ever
take this scene for granted. As I scanned the panorama of
sea and island and beach and headland and cliff top, I was
suddenly made aware that this canvas of God's art had
been added to by us humans. The white cottages along
the shore were a significant part of the beauty. It made me
think: Had God allowed for that? Indeed, had God actually worked that into the picture? Milleniums before the
photographs I would take a few days later on the Rathlin
Island ferry, had He worked in the spaces for the harbor,
the marina, the cottages, and the town that we would add
later? Indeed, had He imagined the detail of the sails of
the yacht that was coming across the bay as I thought
these thoughts? Were we given the privilege of working
it out over time? Were people who had no idea that they
playing a part complicit in something much bigger than
they could ever imagine?

That is in essence what I had been trying to say in this
book. God has left space for human beings to be involved
with Him to deliver truth and beauty and to be engaged in
the questions and answers of how and why and what we
are doing spinning through the universe. You do not need
to be a believer to be involved in the conversation any
more than the sailor needs to go onto the Atlantic Ocean
with the sole purpose of coloring a little flourish on my
seaside scene.

A few days later I was in the Old Museum Arts Theatre
in Belfast listening to the last stanza from William Blake's

hymn, "Jerusalem":

I will not cease from mental fight,
Nor shall my sword sleep in my hand
Till we have built Jerusalem
In England's green and pleasant land.

They were familiar words like so many classic old hymns
that become a part of you without you even being aware
of it. Tonight the words became a blinding light. They gave
me the idea of what this book was about—a month after
it was finished! The hymn was being used as the finale of
the play *Jerusalem, Jerusalem*, written by New Zealand
novelist and playwright Mike Riddell. It is based on the
New Zealand radical poet and mystic, James K. Baxter,
who died in 1972, a man of intrigue who comes across as
a fusion of Jack Kerouac, Charles Manson, and a Christian-
ized Maharishi Yogi! An intensely gripping performance
had my head reeling with the issues of how modern life
clashes with the soul and how we can attempt to find a
way to save ourselves from the deadness that results.

The play left as many questions as answers, which is
something I am learning to appreciate more. My laziness
often causes me to look to God, expecting that He will give
me answers, when actually He is just throwing out the
questions that I need to be wrestling with as a matter of
urgency. As the cast sang this verse in the context of Riddell's play, I got an awakening in the depths of me and a
new urgency of passion to see the world with brilliant new
possibilities. To not "cease" or "sleep" 'till God's kingdom
comes and it is on earth as it is in heaven lit up my heart
with a desire to go out of that theater and into my world
and make sure I give every ounce of my being to be about
the business that Jesus started when He became flesh and
lived among us.

Blake was a poet who prophesied; Baxter was a poet who raged in an attempt to change things from how they were into how they could be; and songwriter Billy Bragg, an English socialist (best known for having recently taken some of Woody Guthrie's words and turning them into songs which were released as *Mermaid Avenue Volumes 1 and 2*) had recorded a protest version of the same hymn— all of this seems appropriate in the light of this book. *The Rock Cries Out* is about one man's attempt to follow Jesus and build His kingdom, "Jerusalem" (in Blake's poetry) here on earth. As this one man has attempted to find out what that looks like and how to be involved in that construction, he has discovered that many of those who prophesy into his dilemma are rock singers, not preachers. And even more incredible than that—they are not even claiming to follow the same Jesus he does. This book isn't just about rock criticism; it's about changing the world.

TWO

THE TIMES THEY ARE A-CHANGING

I have read every book that has ever been written about Bob Dylan, at least every one I ever found in a bookstore, second hand bookstore, or friends' bookshelf! I have had a shelf in my own office that actually collapsed under the weight of Sheldon, Heylin (originals and updates!), Sounes, Scaduto, Ricks, Williams, and the countless others (do not forget about Scott Marshall's *Restless Pilgrim* from Relevant Books). There is a lot of information, a lot of insight, and a lot of conjecture. Sometimes there are even more questions than answers. Maybe that has always been Dylan's intention anyway.

In all the literary professors and academic poets and well-read Dylanophiles, the resource that has sharpened my mind and soul to Dylan's muse the most in recent days has been a criminally unknown singer from east Belfast, Brian Houston.

Houston is a parochial star, but somehow the injustices of rock 'n' roll have left him as our most precious little secret. We don't mind; we get to buy his records and go to his concerts. The rest of you don't know how much you should mind, and what you don't know won't hurt you. He minds because the swimming pool in Malibu still eludes him!

In the days following the outbreak of the 2003 Iraqi War, Belfast, like a host of other cites across the world, held its Peace March. Houston sang "God On Our Side" alongside his own "We Don't Need Religion," and a listener to my radio show thought Dylan had written both. When he sang for another event that my students were holding, he added two more Dylan songs, "The Times They Are A-Changing" and "Masters Of War." In the context of war we were pummelled by the power of their poetry, both those students who knew nothing about Bob Dylan and those of us who had been listening to the originals for decades.

On another occasion, Houston was doing a songwriter circle on my radio show. Along with Nashville's Julie Lee and Queens University student David McNair, they were sharing songs and stories, singing and jamming with each other as songs progressed. I had asked them to do a song that they would sing when the concert was wrapping up, everybody was on their side and they could relax into their biggest hit, a new song that they had just written, and a cover of somebody else's song. When it came time for Houston's cover, he hesitated and pulled out the scribblings he had been jotting down since the show began. He said he had never done this before and simply launched himself off a cliff and into Dylan's "Like A Rolling Stone." A couplet in, I looked at David and Julie, whose mouths and eyes were as wide open as mine. What a risk on live radio? How could he remember the words? Would he make it through? We all stopped breathing and started praying. The relief when he finished was palpable, the respect too huge to contain in the studio.

In the first instance, it was the close proximity to war and in the second, the close proximity to the venomous spittle that accompanies the poetry of the song, but both these instances gave me a heightened awareness of the genius of Bob Dylan's songs and the cutting edge of his prophetic challenge to the world of the early '60s that still lingers in the air loud and clear four decades later. I also began to think that though Dylan's "Christian" albums *Slow Train Coming, Saved,* and *Shot Of Love* were clearer in their understanding and proclamation of evangelical Christianity, they were probably not as prophetic in a biblical sense than those first few years of his epic career. The Old Testament prophets were those who would say it straight and sharp, cutting to the heart of society's injustice and individual selfishness. They were the weird eccentrics on the fringes who sent shockwaves right to the center.

Dylan's Christian trilogy may have been more clearly defined in their Christian polemic, but they were almost like the prophet from the center blowing massaging bubbles to believers on the edges! *Slow Train Coming,* which remains an underrated gem in his canon because of the gospel associations, does challenge the listener as to who is in charge—"Gotta Serve Somebody"—and asks them to wake up to the fact that Karl Marx, Henry Kissinger, and foreign oil are sending us down a road to destruction. Yet the power of the application of his new found Christian faith is blunted by the too obvious formula of his testimony. Songs like "I Believe In You" and "Precious Angel" from *Slow Train Coming* and the entire album *Saved* are as brilliant a song cycle of Christian profession as there has ever been, but in a prophetic sense, they fall short of those early '60s days.

In the early '60s, Bob Dylan changed the possibilities of pop and rock music forever. Single-handedly, he bridged the gap between the folk singers, with their serious wordy songs of protest and folklore, and the pop bands, who navigated love songs that you could shake your body to, to the top of the pop charts. As he came across the bridge, he bumped into The Beatles, and they traded the cultures on each other's sides of the chasm. From there The Beatles got wordy and philosophical and moved from "She Loves You" to "I'm A Loser" to "Taxman" to "Revolution" and beyond. Dylan strapped on an electric guitar and to the shout of "Judas!" meshed the poetry with amplifiers and drums.

Elvis Presley had, of course, with the help of Marlon Brando and James Dean from the world of cinema, been the John The Baptist, making straight the paths for what would seem to be salvation in the form of '60s freedom. The youth that would soon become a definitive age group in itself and a commercial market for the first time in history were looking around at their parents and feeling the constraints of the straightjacket: the shirt and tie, the respectability, the new middle class work ethic, the respectable status quo of traditional values. Bob Dylan and The Beatles were the Messiahs who articulated and smashed to smithereens any remaining chains of parental, ecclesiastical, and traditional values! Maybe no other song expressed the change that was taking place as well as "The Times They Are A-Changing." It was the Sermon On The Mount of a whole new epoch.

When *Uncut* magazine came to chart the forty best Bob Dylan songs and ask musicians and critics alike to choose and comment, writer Ian McDonald described "The Times They Are A-Changing" as "genuine modern broadsheet writing, this epic outburst of the early sixties youth renaissance still thrills with its quasi biblical prophecy of a new era just coming into flower."[1] One of Nick Cave's Bad Seeds, Jim Sclavunos said, "Even early on born again Bob was in full effect, bristling with youthful verve and prophetic wrath, admonishing the elders."[2]

If his early songs cataloged the changes of the time in words, then by 1965 Dylan was ringing in the changes of rock music. As The Beatles were moving away from twenty-five minute pointless screaming live shows to move pop music on with *Rubber Soul* and *Revolver*, Dylan was making more radical and fundamental changes by going electric to screams of a different tone than The Beatles. "Like A Rolling Stone" would take him to number two in the American charts and would take rock music to heights never before dreamed of. The times were really changing now.

Dylan's part in the change cannot be underestimated; Greil Marcus goes as far as to say, "Bob Dylan seemed less to occupy a turning point in cultural space and time than to be the turning point. As if culture would turn according to his wishes or even his whim; the fact was for a long moment it did."[3] Live Aid's instigator and Britain's honorary knight of punk, Bob Geldof speaks about how Dylan affected his youth growing up in the very conservative Dublin, Ireland: "Dylan had scooped the whole of American folk music (folk, blues, country) and married it to the Psalms, the poets, the Old Testament and hurled it at my head, articulating the inchoate urge I was feeling."[4] The question that needs to be asked in response to that is, why were those who lived upon and were called to proclaim the biblical Word to a generation needing connection not meeting Geldof and everybody else's need? Why was Dylan a better divider of truth than those with a vocation to do so?

The most pertinent concerns for those being led into the new territory of the swinging '60s was the threat of nuclear war, the Vietnam War, and civil rights' injustices. Marcus points out that though the folk revival had its springboard in the Kingstown Trio's "Tom Dooley" hit in 1958, it got its moral energy from "something much bigger, more dangerous and more important: the civil rights movement."[5] Ian McDonald rightly says Dylan was like the broadsheet of the time sending out news reports and commentary on the issues of the day.

As The Beatles and The Rolling Stones would move the bodies and have longer haired heads a-shaking, Dylan went for the mind below the hair and the soul within the body.

The elders could not say they had not been warned as "The Times They Are A-Changing" told the mothers and fathers that their world had changed beyond recognition, and if they were not going to get involved in the change they should stand aside; hand over the mantle. Dylan himself could never have known the speed of change that would be ushered in by his own articulation. For those mothers and fathers, rapid change had not been part of their conditioning. Everything was done as it had been, and so they would have real difficulties with all that Dylan was prophesying. For many social commentators, this would be a defining line between the generations. Many would not have the ability to either get out of the way or to lend a hand. This change would be treated with suspicion.

Anthony Scaduto saw it as a warning to "the dinosaurs— writers, critics, politicians—not to stand in the way of the flood waters of change that were engulfing the world."[6] The clergy could easily be added to the list. The Church would be a very fine example of this continental shift between generations. The next four decades would see a crisis within the Church in its broadest sense as the old mind-set tried to deal with the new one. That same youthful energy and impatience that Dylan was the spokesperson for in the wider community were beginning to stretch the old wineskins within Christendom.

It should be no surprise that Dylan would land on the consciousness of music at the train station of social protection. He had traveled from his Duluth home to New York City on the trail of Woody Guthrie because his attempts at phone calls had failed. Guthrie is the musical link in the evolutionary chain from the first half of the twentieth century and the explosion of articulated and topical pop at the end of it. He was the social commentator traveling with three chords and the truth across America. He articulated the reality and suffering of the dust bowl era, highlighting the issues and protesting the injustice. Unbeknown to him, he educated the young Bob Dylan, who would become his successor in the folk singing apostolic succession. He handed him down many artifacts. As well as the social commentary, there were the biblical reference points so alive in Guthrie, who had used Jesus as a role model and inspiration for revolution. U2's cover of Guthrie's "Jesus Christ" on the *Vision Shared: A Tribute To Woody Guthrie* and Leadbelly and Wilco's "Christ For President" from their *Mermaid Avenue* project, where along with Billy Bragg, they put music to the lyrics that Guthrie never got to use, both show a revolutionary side of Jesus so often absent from those who claim to know Him best. There is no doubt Dylan's Jewish roots were also a factor in the use of the Bible in his songs, but the freedom to reference Jesus on songs like "Masters Of War" did not come from his memories of the synagogue.

Dylan's allegiance to the civil rights movement probably had its origins in Woody Guthrie's *Bound For Glory* memoirs—"I could see men of all colors bouncing along in the boxcar."[7] Guthrie's kingdom was one that broke down class and race barriers. Though in practical terms, Dylan came to the civil rights movement through his two-year stormy relationship with Suze Rotolo, who graces the front of *Freewheelin' Bob Dylan*. Rotolo's mother was involved with the unions, and Suze supported Congress On Racial Equality (CORE), going on marches for civil rights. Though he had been in the slipstream of Woody Guthrie musically for a while, this was his introduction to social protest. He wrote "The Death Of Emmet Til" with Rotolo's informed guidance, and it opened the floodgates for two years of journalistic political commentary songs. Linda Solomon would review the Rotolo inspired *Freewheelin'*, "He stands outside his problems and writes a credo for people to live by. The emotional understatement in his voice emphasizes the power of his lyrics and his genuine concern for the state of the world."[8]

The state of the world had never been worse. It is not exaggerating to say that the planet had been dangled over the edge of oblivion. Dylan wrote "A Hard Rain's A-Gonna Fall" as a direct result of the Cuban missile crisis. Tensions between Kennedy and Castro over a two-year period reached a crisis that threatened the entire world as Kruschev and Kennedy had an "eyeball to eyeball," as Kennedy described it. Dylan has said that the song was written in a state of panic that the number of songs he would get the chance to write was threatened by the imminent end of the world, and so he wrote as many as he could in the one apocalyptic stream of powerful couplets that created the sense of fearful darkness that the world was in for a few days at the end of 1962. In *Back Pages*, Andy Gill describes it as "the closest folk music had come to the Revelation of St. John, and every bit as scary."[9]

The world survived, and so it was back to the aid of Martin Luther King Jr. Here was a minister of religion becoming an icon of the '60s. Long before Dylan joined the Vineyard Church's Bible study that was so widely publicized during his Christian conversion period of 1979 and 1980, he was working with a church leader to bring about the justice that the Bible preaches so much about. Sadly, the white Church was not in tow. Indeed, the Church was an instigator of segregation. The grotesque and unbelievable hypocrisy is put well by a master of philosophy student at our university, who wrote, "The Southern Baptist Convention, an all-white body, sent millions of dollars to Africa for mission, yet barred Africans living in America with membership."[10]

Martin Luther King Jr. had been disappointed with the Church's support of his campaigning. Indeed, while he thought they should be his strongest allies, most were in direct opposition. For King, this was a crux issue for the

credibility of the Church's place in the society of this day.
He would be strong enough to warn "that if the Church does
not stop uttering its 'pious irrelevancies and sanctimonious
trivialities,' then it will, 'be dismissed as an irrelevant social
club with no meaning for the twentieth century.'"[11]

How many times and in how many places has the Church
taken the road of status quo, a pastoring of the way things
are rather than a prophetic voice of how things ought to and
can be? As Northern Ireland became in the '70s and '80s, so
the deep southern states of America were in the '50s and
'60s. Here were places where the cross and resurrection of
Jesus could have been proven to the doubters and the cynics
by those who truly believed in what the first Easter had
achieved. If they had taken the power of Christ's passion and
then lived out the words that He taught about loving enemies
and peacemaking, they could have been a shop window for
the validity of Christianity around the world. Instead, they
maintained the divided societies that allowed the world to
ignore Christianity as the contributing factor to wars and
horrific injustices.

The Bible has constant warnings to the Church about her
role in society and the danger of spiritualizing the faith into
a religious and pious ghetto. In the Old Testament prophecy
of Amos, God would in no uncertain terms highlight what His
priorities for the community of faith are:

"I hate, I despise your religious feasts;
I cannot stand your assemblies. Even though you bring me
burnt offerings
And grain offerings
I will not accept them.
Though you bring me choice offerings
I will have no regard for them. Away with the noise of your
songs!
I will not listen to the music of your harps.

But let justice roll on like a river, righteousness like a never-failing stream!"[12]

Yet, the Church seems to ignore such clear biblical mandates and spends resources and all her efforts in religious events and conferences, rather than seeking that justice and righteousness in the world around them. Many times passages like these are wished away by spiritualizing the meaning and somehow ignoring the reality of Amos' context of very clear social inequalities. Particularly in evangelical circles, the vast crusades of Billy Graham were held in reverential awe at the same time when Martin Luther King Jr.'s nonviolent campaign to bring justice were deemed at least liberal and at worst something near demonic. A look in the mirror of the scriptures of Amos might have redressed the balance in what was perceived to have been the most biblical of the two very different campaigns of Graham and King in the late '50s and '60s. In 1958, King urged Graham not to allow himself to be used by Governor Price Daniels, a segregationist, the Governor of Texas, in his re-election bid. Graham's right-hand man would write to King and say that Billy Graham never gets involved in politics. Thirty years after King's murder, Graham would speak of King as "the most eloquent spokesperson of the Civil Rights Movement, a champion of justice for all people ..."[13] Sad that he could not have stood with someone he so admired!

As King's brothers in Christ kept him at arm's length, Bob Dylan filled the gap—the (rock) folkies cried out! He sang "Blowing In The Wind" and "Only A Pawn In Their Game" at the Washington rally in August 1963 when King made his legendary "I Have A Dream" speech. Others to perform included Dylan's lover at that moment, Joan Baez, Peter Paul And Mary, who had brought him to the wider audience with their version of "Blowing In The Wind," and the legendary Mahalia Jackson. It had been Jackson who inspired King's iconoclastic speech by shouting, "Tell us your dream,

Martin!" King had indeed begun his speech by alerting the listener to the significance of the day that he said "will go down in history as the greatest demonstration for freedom in the history of our nation."

Indeed, Andy Gill would go as far as to say that King was one of the connections in Dylan that drew him to understand the power of the Bible. He writes, "He has always been keenly aware of biblical discourse as a useful storehouse of mythopoeic folk imagery, littering his songs with references to parables and prophets; and as he got involved with the civil rights movement, Dylan surely recognized the commitment of church leaders like Martin Luther King Jr., and the strength King's followers drew from their faith. Indeed, many of his songs from this period suggest his acknowledgement that protest anthems are, in effect secular hymns, and his delivery frequently takes on a sermonizing cast."[14]

Clinton Heylin would also wax lyrical about Dylan's Bible knowledge. Writing about how the discovery of the poet Robert Graves in England and the French impressionists Rimbaud, Baudelaire, and Verlaine had widened Dylan's lyrical potential he goes on, "However the most important literary resource for this lapsed Jew remained the Bible."[15] He then shows how "When The Ship Comes In" reveals knowledge of apocalyptic tracts of the Old Testament and how he uses Jesus' words in Matthew's Gospel as the crucial line in "The Times They Are A-Changing": "so the last will be first and the first will be last."[16]

The white churches of the day were not hearing so many sermons on the subject. Quite how the brutal cruelty both physical and emotional that black people were suffering from horrific injustices could be ignored by the white Church leaders of the day is too obscene to believe, and yet the Church has to constantly be asking itself what are our contemporary blind spots. Martin Luther King Jr. would warn against the insipid maintenance of the status quo by churches citing the example of Jeremiah. "Jeremiah is a shining example of the truth that religion should never sanction the status quo. This more than anything else should be inculcated into the minds of modern religionists, for the worst disservice that we as individuals or churches can do to Christianity is to become sponsors and supporters of the status quo. How often has religion gone down, chained to a status quo it allied itself with."[17] Race may not be the burning issue that it was forty years ago, though the demonic strains of prejudice and bigotry are still alive and well in many church pews and more tragically pulpits, but what about capitalism, materialism, and the third world debt and trade laws that maintain their status quo? The reality is that the three richest men in the world have more power over wealth than the sixty poorest countries, and the Church ignores the righteous anger to maintain the status quo.

Peter Yarrow would later say, "The March on Washington was a pivotal and critical day because it was so filled with an energy—a positive energy of decency and goodness and belief in ourselves and one another—that you could just scoop it up." Certainly it shifted the movement up a few gears. Again we need to ask why the white churches did not see what Yarrow could see, both the goodness of such a day and more vitally the utter biblical mandate of such a day. In a letter he wrote to white church leaders from a Birmingham jail four months before the "I Have A Dream" stage, King pinpointed his disappointment with his white church colleagues. In their nonviolent protests against segregation in Alabama, King got little support from white churches. Indeed, some ministers told their people that to get involved would be breaking the law. Unjust laws were to be kept and heinous immoral segregation tolerated! Christians were, he said, "more cautious than courageous and have remained silent behind the anesthetizing security of stained glass windows … In the midst of blatant injustices inflicted upon the Negro,

I have watched white churchmen stand on the sideline and mouth pious irrelevancies and sanctimonious trivialities ... Is organized religion too inextricably bound to the status quo to save the nation and our world?"[18]

If we are looking for some reason why Dylan did not go the way of his best Beatle friend George Harrison on a spiritual journey to India but found his front page news conversion as the fulfilment of his Jewish roots in the Christian Messiah, there may be a reason in that while Harrison was brought up in at best a dull dutiful Liverpudlian Catholicism or at worst a completely Christian free zone of England, then Dylan would probably have found it incredibly difficult not to have carried with him the prophetic and radically social transformation of Martin Luther King Jr.'s passionate biblical preaching.

The 1963 Newport Folk Festival was the height of the folk revival, at least in its marriage to civil rights. Gill calls it "Dylan's coronation,"[19] but it has to be said that it was also the "Dear Sir," of his abdication letter. On that July weekend, he was being covered, or name-dropped, continually and, as well as performing in his own slot, duetted with Joan Baez. His set would have the *Newport News* describe him as "the voice of the oppressed in America and the champion of the little man."[20] The finale would be described by David Hajdu as a defining moment. Singing "We Shall Overcome" with Baez, Pete Seeger, Peter, Paul and Mary, Theo Bikel, and The SNCC (The Student Non-violent Coordinating Committee) Freedom Singers, everyone holding hands, Hajdu writes, "The image of this assemblage at Newport would become one of the primary symbols of the 1960's folk revival; the old guard joined with the new, the commercial and the communist, black and white, leading a sea of young people in a sing-along for freedom."

Soon after his final recordings of these two prolific protest years, Dylan would be off like a rolling stone carrying no political moss as he headed to a more defining moment in his career and in modern culture. Twelve months later he would be back at Newport, but this time his songs were about relationships and caused the editor of *Sing Out* to suggest he had lost contact with people. By 1965, he had certainly lost contact with the Newport people altogether as he did his first performance with a band, and even some of those he held hands with twenty-four months previous were confused and incensed by how loud and unfolky Dylan had become. Even though Newport was about blues as well as folk, Dylan had changed the times again.

Dylan's haste at leaving behind the folk revival and the songs of social provocation has asked serious questions about the seriousness of his commitment. In 1965 he would even disown his protest songs, refuse to sing them and suggest he had only written topical songs to get into the magazine *Broadside* and to further his career.[20] Joan Baez would say that she never remembers him marching or doing any civil disobedience, but neither did she believe him when he said he wrote those song for the money.[21]

The truth is that Dylan moved on with the times that were a-changing and merely redirected his prophecy. There would still be protest, and his songs on behalf of justice for George Jackson and Hurricane Carter would have race issues at their core. Joe Klein put it well in his biography *Woody Guthrie: A Life*, "Dylan was very much his own man from the start. He never really had any political goals—just a personal vision."[22]

The protest was simply given a whole new canvas as he stepped out of that journalistic phase to become an impressionistic painter poet of the new world coming on. His folk revival buddies were simply left in a side alley as Dylan took to the Main Street to shout his rage at the heart of the culture. In many ways he didn't just take a walk down Main Street; he rebuilt it.

Dylan might have been the political spokesman for a few very worthy causes, but when he added electric guitar to his sound, he took on the spiritual issues of his entire generation and jumped into the vortex of the musical revolution. As The Beatles came toward him in the lyricism of their mid-'60s albums, so he headed out toward them and pasted his literary poetry onto a rock 'n' roll band. *Highway 61 Revisited* and *Rubber Soul* and then *Blonde On Blonde* and *Revolver* were simply iconic moments in the history of pop and rock. They did not write or work together, and they recorded in different continents, but these albums are collaborations in spirit. What they did for everything that would come after was to open up the possibilities of the ten-year-old genre that is rock 'n' roll. Anything was possible in sound and in topic and content.

Dylan spoke of having given up when he returned to America after the English tour that had been captured in the documentary *Dont Look Back* (sic). He went to Woodstock with his wife Sara and it seems began to think of poetry and novels and reinvention. Paul Williams sees this time as being "like Christ after going to the desert, he had passed a turning point,"[23] and an entirely new kind of artist emerged to change the world, quite literally. Dylan himself put it, "Last spring I guess I was going to stop singing. I was very drained. I was playing a lot of songs I didn't want to play. I was singing songs I really didn't want to sing. But 'Like A Rolling Stone' changed it all."[24] Oh, did it change it all.

It was six minutes long in a world of the two-and-a-half-minute single and it was his biggest hit to date. Without it, it is doubtful if any of this book could have been written. It was what Greil Marcus was talking about when he said that Dylan changed the entire culture by his own whim. What was it about, and who? Who knows? It did express the lostness of a generation and most probably Dylan himself, who were now a few years into those times that were are a-changing, and they were out there on their own with no direction home. It is one thing to head out into unknown territory, but when you do, there is no one there to give you directions or guidance or help you make sense of it.

This was Dylan trying to make sense of all that was going on around him. In a few very short years, fashion had become the fashion, music had become the soul of society, and The Beatles were more popular than Jesus. The times had a-changed at unprecedented speed and with all kinds of possible consequences. "Something was happening," and the truth is that Mr. Jones, whoever he might have been in "Ballad Of A Thin Man," was not the only one who "don't know what it is." At this point neither of the Moses figures of Dylan and The Beatles leading the youth through to the Promised Land had a clue what they were party to or what that land was going to look like. They only knew that their Egypt was long behind them.

The obvious response from those who Dylan had told to get out of the way because they could not lend a hand would be to point the finger and say that this was a generation reaping what they sowed. Yet who is reaping? Who sowed? There was a lost generation needing a direction home. The times a-changed, and no one listened to the prophecy and adjusted their spiritual or social position to be able to respond. Without direction, the tide would surge to Woodstock via visits to the Maharishi Yogi aided by psychedelic drugs, free love, and near anarchical living. Dylan would find himself seeking sense in a great many places, from rural Woodstock to family life to a conversion to born again Christianity to touring the world endlessly. A rolling stone indeed!

THREE

SMELLS LIKE ECCLESIASTES

I t was a JFK moment—or, for the under-thirties, a 9/11 moment. I remember exactly where I was and who I was with. I had spent the day in Dublin with my friend Cole, who happened to be over from London to write an article for *Propoganda*, the official U2 fanzine. We were all still standing in the middle of the living room when I switched on MTV to be met with the news that Kurt Cobain was dead. I was not a Nirvana fan, though my friends were, and I had taken on a new sense of admiration with their *MTV Unplugged* performance. We sat down with a deep sense of sadness. Though not a fan, I knew he was a prestigious talent, and more than that, he was for sure the spokesman of the generation.

The sense of shock and loss was only added to by my sense of inevitability. There was something almost written in stone that said this had to be. His life, his music, his fame, and his inability to deal with the life that had been thrust upon him led to some kind of obvious conclusion: suicide, rock martyrdom, and the birth of a legend to take his place with Jim Morrison, Sid Vicious, Jimi Hendrix, et al, "that silly club," his mother had tried to convince him not to join. As I stood there paralyzed by the enormity of it all, my mind was immediately drawn to the book of Ecclesiastes. It was as though we were watching the dramatic acting out of that biblical book of wisdom where the preacher in Jerusalem wrote: "Meaningless, meaningless, all is meaningless."[1]

The book of Ecclesiastes is actually the first rock concept album ever written. It would have made a great concept album for Nirvana, and the bulk of it has been written and rewritten many times in the fifty-year history of rock 'n' roll. If it was recorded, it would be impossible to take a song out of context. It cannot be dipped into here and there, but has to be read as an entire thesis to find its conclusion. The writer of the book basically sets out to find where the meaning of life might lie and makes his conclusions. He looks in pleasure and in education and in good deeds and in wealth and concludes that all these things are meaningless.

From this early declaration of how meaningless everything is, the next number of verses is the weariest passage in the entire canon of the Judeo-Christian Scriptures. Like an Irish weather forecast, the rain falls into rivers that flow into the sea and then rise as clouds, only to fall as rain into rivers that flow into the sea and then rise as clouds ... Everything is so tedious and repetitive to the conclusion "all things are wearisome more than one can say."[2] There is nothing new under the sun, so what is the point of perpetuating the cycle?

Douglas Coupland wrote the modern version of this in his 1992 novel, *Life After God*. Setting out to see what "post God" American life looks like, he gets a little frightened, "I was wondering what the logical end product of this recent business of my feeling less and less. Is feeling nothing the inevitable end result of believing in nothing? And then I got to feeling frightened—thinking that there might be not actually be anything to believe in, in particular. I thought it would be such a sick joke to have to remain alive for decades and not believe in or feel anything."[3] A sick joke indeed. Who needs a life like this? Kurt Cobain didn't.

The Nirvana story is incredibly short. From the release of *Nevermind* with little indication of the success that lay ahead (though signing to Geffen from independent Sub Pop suggests that someone somewhere knew something might be afoot), to the moment Cobain ended his recording career and birthed by death the legend with a bullet to his head was less than thirty-one months. There were only two official studio albums to add to Sub Pop's earlier release, *Bleach*, plus a compilation of outtakes. There was the obligatory early '90s unplugged album that was released posthumously, as was another live full-on grunge album *From The Muddy Banks Of The Wishkah*. In that short time, Nirvana literally became the biggest band on the planet, leap frogging the U2s and the REMs to the top of every rock magazine poll and chart.

They married the attitude of punk to the guitar edge of heavy rock and then laid out over that these great pop melodies, topped with the Cobain grunge growl. "The Guns 'n' Roses that it is okay to like" Britain's *NME* said. It was loud, it was physical, and it was angst-fueled. If you were a teenager as the early '90s set off toward millennium apocalypse, then Nirvana was the perfect sonic comfort blanket. The generation that had watched their parents split up and been bounced around from one to the other or rejected by one or the other was reaping the harvest, near famine, of the breakdown of family life. They had stood in the gap in the covert wars between those who should have been building their security. They were weighed down in guilt and emotional baggage that

31 | THREE

they had experienced much earlier in their lives than the generations before them. Michael Jackson was no catharsis, so that first time they heard the riff of "Smells Like Teen Spirit," their fraying little souls must have sensed relief; a spokesman has arrived from God, and they knocked the aforementioned Jackson off the number one slot!

Their success, though, was yet one more contradiction to add to the whole world of contradictions that fired that Nirvana grunge sound. Though there are many clues in Cobain's songs to his despondent life and slide toward that tragic end, it is not the lyrics that defined him as a spokesman for the generation the way you might find with a Dylan, a Lennon, a Springsteen, or a Rotten. The generation that Nirvana freed from Michael Jackson et al did not need fancy literary articulation of their alienation. This was the generation that, having grown up under a visual bombardment of media messages, had skipped from the left side to the right side of the brain and therefore were in need of few words of explanation or confessional exorcism. This lot needed an experience, and grunge gave them the happening that released all the pain and guilt and shame. Crowd surfing gave some kind of anarchic connection. There was some communal sharing taking place that had been missed in the broken home or the outmoded Church. Here was a place and a crowd and a sound to give some meaning.

Kurt Cobain was an accident waiting to happen. He was an angst hero waiting to happen too. The first line of "Serve The Servants," the opening track of *In Utero* (the follow-up to the surprise and phenomenally successful *Nevermind* album) begins by Cobain suggesting his "teenage angst has paid off." But Cobain's was no manufactured angst to sell records. Sadly, he never got the chance to get old. Six months before he shot himself, *Q* magazine's Phil Sutcliffe spoke of delving "into Kurt Cobain's curious world of heroin abuse, acute paranoia, wilful self-destruction, shoulder shrugging nihilism and child-like love."[4]

Nothing much had gone right for Cobain. He seems to have been a pleasant enough boy, but his parent's separation screwed him up big time. He also had a stomach complaint that would later find its only relief in heroine. That his birth was in the dead-end logging town of Aberdeen, Washington state, was another piece of bad luck that in the end turned out to be the luckiest thing of all, or unluckiest, depending on your take on the fame that Kurt Cobain enjoyed or endured. For some reason, Seattle would become the Liverpool of early '90s pop. It would be the place where a little label called Sub Pop would help give the world grunge rock, and the king of that genre in the history of music would be Kurt Cobain and his band Nirvana.

In his suicide note, Cobain said, "Since the age of seven I've become hateful of all humans in general."[5] This is obviously a reference to his parents breaking up around that time. It would seem in just a general glance across the photographs of his life that there is a huge difference in the innocent and secure smiling kid and the pained pop star. His mother would say that "it just destroyed his life. He changed completely. He became really sullen, kind of mad and always frowning and ridiculing."

It seems that the rock cries out across America about the end product of the breakdown of the family unit. The last half of the twentieth century saw an increase in divorce. We live in a postmodern age where it seems very narrow minded and archaic to ask people who are not in love to live together and refuse them the opportunity to try again. Indeed, the very definition of love is in need of a serious look. It is probably when some warm and fuzzy feeling that is no more than infatuation and set in stone by Hollywood movies that has grown into something a little more realistic that leads lovers to move on! Yet, marriage is not only about the pleasure of the

man or woman; it is about the wellbeing of the one to whom
promises have been made, and once children arrive, there is
an even bigger responsibility. Marriage may be an outdated
institution and the family unit may be archaic, but the reality
is that there is a very close correlation between the success of
the family unit and the wellbeing of children into adulthood.

Cobain's troubles were not just nurture. Nature had fated that
he would suffer from a chronic stomach complaint for many
years. The medical world could not seem to find any solutions
to the daily pain. His physical ailments were not helped by
the music. He told Jon Savage, "My body is damaged from
music in two ways. I have a red irritation in my stomach. It's
psychosomatic, caused by all the anger and screaming. I have
scoliosis, where the curvature of your spine is bent, and the
weight of my guitar has made it worse. I'm always in pain
and that adds to the anger of our music. I'm grateful to it, in a
way."[6] His stomach problems may have been caused by the
prescribing of Ritalin to the young Cobain to counteract his
hyperactive behavior.

The Ritalin might have been an abusive use of drugs from
legal sources, but it was a huge addition to the Cobain tragedy
waiting to happen when he looked toward illegal drugs to
relieve the pain. Heroine probably proved a fatal addition to
the molotov cocktail of physical circumstances that would
explode in one twenty-seven-year-old life. His journals
released eight years after his death give some insight into the
truth of the rumors of his perpetual battle with heroine. On a
Madrid hotel notepaper weeks before his death, he tells his
private daily diary that though he scoffed at the idea that you
could get hooked on heroine after one trip, "I now believe
this to be very true."[7] With all the different pains that raged in
Cobain's body, it is hard to know where he could find a way
out.

It is a very sad and despairing story captured in that one

most famous photograph where Cobain is sitting on the floor with his hand on his forehead, the pain in his face so graphic that it is a unique shot in the history of rock 'n' roll. Ian Tilton from the late great U.K. music paper, *Sounds*, took the photograph. *Q* magazine included it, without surprise, in "The 100 Greatest Rock 'n' Roll Photographs," and Tilton explains the scene surrounding it. It was actually taken almost exactly one year before the Nirvana tornado went hurtling on the release of "Smells Like Teen Spirit." Sounds were ahead of the game, and Tilton got total access to a gig in Seattle. He says, "At the end, he trashed his equipment then came off the back of the stage pumped with adrenaline, and that energy and emotion has to go somewhere. I followed him right behind, back where the audience couldn't see, and he just sat down and cried for about thirty seconds. He was aware I was there, but it didn't bother him that I took the photograph. The band also accepted him crying, so it was probably something he'd done before."[8] After Cobain's death, it became the one picture that really told the entire story. No other photograph has ever captured the pain of a life quite like Tilton's.

When asked about the reason for Cobain taking himself out of the story, biographer Christopher R. Cross answered, "I would rank some of the top reasons as 1) the hopelessness of addiction; 2) constant pain from his stomach; 3) emotional pain; and 4) the delusional effects of the combination of all the drugs he was on. But those would just be the tip of the iceberg—I hope my book helps explain this more. Though, as I write in the introduction, it is ultimately a spiritual question, not one of fact."[9] In that introduction for *Heavier Than Heaven*, Cross yearns to find answers to what went on after Cobain purchased the suicide weapon. "They are questions concerning spirituality, the role of madness in artistic genius, the ravages of drug abuse on the soul, and the desire to understand the chasm between the inner and the outer man."[10]

Certainly fame was no answer for the wellbeing in Kurt Cobain's soul and indeed in many ways exacerbated his problems. It gave him the money to indulge in drugs and increased the contradictions of underground and world domination that was Nirvana's career. In their video, *Live Tonight Sold Out*, Cobain made it clear that he never wanted or envisaged doing arena shows. Success was neither a desire nor a seeming possibility when Nirvana started. They were lovers of the underground. That was their mission, and yet, here they were, the biggest band on the planet. Meteoric was a word that could have been coined to describe the Nirvana phenomenon. Cobain was so fragile and screwed up that the chances of him surviving the ride upon that meteor were slim. It could have been the salvation from his past. Instead it added to the pain of his past and became an emotional cocktail that became far too great to find healing from.

There is always a fatal mistake that goes down within the Christian mind-set: that those who are not Christians are not happy. They will say, "Look at that Justin Timberlake. All that money. All those houses. All those yachts. All those fast cars. All those fast girls! But do you think that he is happy?" Well, of course he is happy! The Bible gives us a hint at such sensory happiness in the very first Eden story. As Eve looked at that first momentary thrill that would cause a fair degree of aftereffects, that fruit looked good and tasted good![11]

So success is an addictive rush. It could indeed be described as the opium of the people. Not for Kurt Cobain though. He would give the distinct impression that he had an aversion to success. It was not what he became a musician for, and when it came, it was unexpected and made the mess that his life was already in too unbearable. The backbone (my use of the word could not be more inappropriate) of his suicide note was that he had not enjoyed music for a long time, that unlike Freddie Mercury, he got no enjoyment from the adoration of the crowd, and that he could not fake it any more. It was his success that he was blaming for the immediate reasons for what his wife would call the betrayal of all who loved him.

Cobain and his cohorts David Grohl and Chris Novoselic detested the late '80s American rock excess and success. Bands like Extreme and Guns N' Roses came in for specific public denouncement. Nirvana had a punk sensibility and inhabited the underground. With the sound Nirvana had, there seemed to be little chance of them becoming anything more than a cult band. No one had any expectations that things would explode the way that they would. When their meteor exploded in September 1991, no one—least of all Kurt Cobain—expected it. So to move from being the slacker among the slackers to being the rich boy in an exclusive big home on Lake Washington was a huge transformation to deal with. If you had wanted it, then maybe you would have found the psychological skills necessary, but if you felt guilty that you had betrayed your people and your original vision, then it was going to be nigh impossible to deal with.

Nirvana had been about music and not sales. In retrospect, it is easy to suggest that they compromised this ideal by producing *Nevermind* for a mass market, but the truth is that at the time, *Nevermind* was no formula for chart success. It did not follow the formula; it blew up the formula and rewrote history. Yes, the Beatlesque sheen that Cobain added to his Black Flag noise did assure him of a little more recognition, and he could not deny he wanted that, but he could never have foreseen the millions of units he would shift. So with *In Utero*, the much anticipated follow-up, he would show Radiohead a few tricks for how to follow huge success with something a little less accessible to help them deal with their chart expectations at the decade's end. Nirvana set out to produce a raw, harsher-sounding album that would certainly disturb the vast majority of the *Nevermind* audience. At the same time, having used Cobain's hero Steve Albini, famous for his work with the Pixies, to gain this rawness, they later brought Scott Litt in to remix "Heart Shaped Box" and "All Apologies" to make them more radio-friendly.

Yet, this is not the entire story. Nirvana was a band and Cobain a writer who were constantly throwing up contradictions. There would be blatant self confession in "Very Ape" that he was "buried" in his contradictions and lies. Charles R. Cross speaks of Cobain's contradictions when it comes to "death wish/death fear." He writes, "Here was a man who never drove over the speed limit and bought a Volvo because he read it was the safest car in the world, while at the same time he recklessly overused heroine to such a degree that overdoses became commonplace in his house."[12]

Another biographer, Christopher Sandford, is cynical about Cobain's disdain for success. He laughs at those who suggest that Cobain held some standard of avoidance of the rock star success game. In his opinion, "His whole approach to performance was a scream for attention. It must have been galling to have achieved his ambition and realized that it still wasn't enough. He could be ecstatic, and experience the brief illumination of happiness. What Kurt Cobain never knew was contentment."[13]

That takes us back to the book of Ecclesiastes. To become famous is no solution either. "There is no remembrance of men of old and even those to come will not be remembered by those who follow."[14] Pop music proves the point in so many artists who are top of the pops for what Andy Worhol would coin "their fifteen minutes of fame" and then would be completely forgotten—who remembers Rick Astley? Maybe Cobain had lost feeling and belief and was thus not prepared to live the sick joke any longer. Douglas Coupland's conclusion in *Life After God* is interesting for a modern novelist. "Now here is my secret: I tell it to you with an openness of heart that I doubt I shall ever achieve again, so I pray that you are in a quiet room as you hear these words.

My secret is that I need God ..."[15] It seems pretty much like Ecclesiastes to me. Maybe there really is nothing new under the sun. We all need to look above it.

As Chuck Swindoll, in his book *Living On The Ragged Edge*, draws from Ecclesiastes chapter one, anything that is done underneath the sun is completely pointless. Only when life is seen from above the sun in God's perspective do we get to shed some meaning on the whole darn thing that we call life. The writer of Ecclesiastes concludes right at the end of chapter twelve that the secret is God. We need a vertical to make sense of the horizontal.

St. Paul wrote about this relationship between the vertical and the horizontal in his letter to the Corinthians. He said, "So we fix our eyes, not in what is seen but what is unseen, for what is seen is temporary but what is unseen is eternal."[16] Jesus, too, thought we should look above the confines of our time: "Do not store up for yourselves treasure on earth, where moth and rust destroy, and where thieves break in and steal. But store up for yourselves treasures in heaven, where moth and rust do not destroy, and where thieves do not break in and steal. For where your treasure is, there your heart will be also."[17]

It is very easy to imprison our lives into the walls of our time and perspectives. It is as though we find the circumstances and limitations of what we can see and understand to close in upon us, causing us to lose hope and be left in the despair of no belief and thus no escape. Bono and U2 called it getting "stuck in a moment you can't get out of" and wrote it for their close friend, Michael Hutchence, who also took his own life. Kurt Cobain was a Generation X icon and spokesman who carried the problems of his day. Having lost all faith in modernity with its old and failed promise of a better world through human achievement, and finding little hope in the future that had been damaged by most of the so-called progress of modernity's technological affects, there was only one thing for it, and Jesus put it as poetically as any Nirvana lyric: "Take life easy, eat, drink and be merry."[18] Without a root in the past or a direction in the future, Cobain was left without a story. There was nothing new under the sun. There was no point. Nothing worked, and if everything failed, so what?

Any reader of Nirvana's work or press would have been quick to see the inevitability of Cobain's early exit. From the repeated line, *No, I don't have a gun*, on "Come As You Are," the song that was supposed to be the big hit on *Nevermind* before "Smells Like Teen Spirit" got there first, to "I Hate Myself and Want To Die" being a leading contender for the title track of *In Utero*, to the photo shoot, where he posed with the barrel of a rifle in his mouth, there were many heavy clues to Cobain's obsessions. He even called one of his fifteen-year-old short movies *Kurt Cobain Commits Bloody Suicide*. These were not the prophecies of someone looking on. These were statements by the man himself! He might have denied the seriousness of the remarks and actually claimed that the *I Hate Myself And Want To Die* title was dropped because people would not get the joke, but most people were perceptive enough to see behind the "joke" to the sadness that was slowly destroying Kurt Cobain's soul.

Like the generation who heard their own pain in the larynx-ripping squall of his grunge sound, Kurt Cobain seemed to be someone who could empathize with them in their purposelessness, weakness, confusion, worthlessness, and shame. That is exactly what Jesus came to do, to sympathize with us in our weakness.[19] Exactly a year after his death, four fans from Toronto drove all the way to Seattle to hang themselves as a tribute to their hero. That Friday one year later just happened to be Good Friday.

FOUR

LIVING IN THE MATERIAL WORLD

I t is a throwaway near doodle become cartoon. A pencil
sketched skyline in the background and a signpost
marked "Bullsh– Avenue." A face with a bubble coming
from the mouth that says GOD-GOD-GOD and underneath
in brackets "a voice cry's in the wilderness." It is so quick a
scribble that the "cry's" is spelled wrong, but in its seeming
haste, it is not only a succinct picture of the last and title track
of George Harrison's posthumously released *Brainwashed*
album, but is a perceptive and accurate conclusion to his
entire solo career and the last forty years of his life.

Brainwashed was the album that Harrison died before
completing, but he had left instructions with his son Dhani
and friend and producer Jeff Lynne on how he wanted it to
sound. In the end it is George Harrison's last statement to the
world. As always it is not as lyrically smooth as his late mate

John, nor as melodically sweet as his old pal Paul, but it has spadefulls (to use a George gardening term!) more spirituality, humor, and integrity than his more esteemed former colleagues. There is that familiar quirkiness to Harrison's poetry. He uses clumsy words that no one else would even attempt, and yet he can come up with a few cracking rhyming couplets, and overall, the content is so personal and conversational that words are just a vehicle to saying so much more.

On "Pisces Fish," we are led into a false sense of idyllic security in the opening line as we find rowers on the river no doubt near Harrison's Henley home. Seconds later we are shaking our heads to rewind the next line and then are smashed across the cerebral ear with that dry wit that wakens the soul from dreaming as we are graphically kept up to date with some geese going to their open air rest room at the river's edge. You've got to smile, and then we are led into similar pastoral images, ending up with chains tangled around cranks and the bell ringers tangled in their rope. The conclusion of the sermon is the need for serenity to find that which lies beneath the madness of our world.

That too has been the Harrison bee in the bonnet since he discovered Eastern mysticism in the mid-'60s and found some way of chanting his way beyond the material world to find some peace on earth. As his last will and testimony, we are treated to lots of God in the mix. Indeed, there is little else that has any consequence. The album begins with him trying to navigate through the filth and grime built up on the walls of life and rightly suggesting we need some kind of destination to aim for or else we end up with no idea of where we are heading and "Any Road" will do.

We end with more blatant exposure of the dirt and the grime as Harrison shows us that he didn't cut himself off completely from the real world in his Henley-On-Thames "Crackerbox

Palace" as he lists the accused who have brainwashed us and
switched off our spiritual lights. Again his answer is God, and
we eventually get a reading from *How To Know God (The Yoga
Aphorisms of Patanjali)* and a chant seemingly called "Namah
Parvati" performed along with Dhani. It is the perfect end to
a final album of the man who took the world to the feet of the
Maharishi and became Krishna's most famous convert. As
someone who follows another faith, I have to agree with his
diagnosis if the medicine I take is from a different bottle.

When Harrison sang about our being brainwashed and about
the dirt and the grime of "Bullsh– Avenue," he always felt he
had a clearer insight than most into all that was awry with the
material world. After his revelation as to the delusional nature
of the materialist solutions to humanity's ultimate questions,
he spent the rest of his life seeking for a more satisfying
insight: the pursuit of God and truth. Though a "rock" singer
more than a "soul" singer, he was very much a singer for the
soul. For him the finding and caring and nurturing of the soul
was what he was on the planet to do and would be the thing
that would last when his time on this planet was through.

Before he changed his soul, George Harrison had already
changed the world. On that day when he passed away on
November 30, 2001, there was that immediate outpouring of
glowing obituaries that the death of a pop idol brings. In some
ways the fuss was a little surprising. When his Beatle pal John
Lennon was shot dead in New York City some twenty-one
years earlier, The Beatles had only been split up ten years.
Lennon too seemed the most popular Beatle, the working
class hero, the half of the Lennon/McCartney songwriting
phenomenon at the very soul of The Beatle's success.
Harrison was always seen as the quiet Beatle, third in the
pecking order, and dying thirty-one years after the band's
split and thirty years after his short-lived solo success; would
the world be all that interested?

The public response to Harrison's passing said much again about the place The Beatles hold in music and social history of the latter part of the twentieth century. It also led in many quarters to a reassessment of Harrison's contribution to that historical impact. Yes, there is little doubt that the reassessment was triggered by the sentimentality of how we honor people in death, but with the excuse of a little more microscopic look at Harrison's achievements and contribution, many things were turned up that in some ways need to be acknowledged not only in The Beatle's story, but in the revolution that was the 1960s and beyond.

The cultural revolution of the swinging '60s was like a quantum leap of nature. Within years, months, weeks even, the entire fabric of Western society was simply knocked so out of kilter that it was unrecognizable from its most recent history. Pop music brought to us by Elvis Presley exploded from its alleyway and reconstructed the entire horizon of history. As with music and fashion, so ideals and values were turned on their heads. A sexual revolution was maybe the most obvious outworking of a hedonistic mind-set that had the teen world by the throat. The philosophy of live fast, enjoy it, and die young was made flesh.

The Beatles epitomized the transformation, and their story is maybe the most remarkable in pop history. In seven short years of recording, they released twenty-two singles, twelve albums, thirteen EPs, four movies, and a TV special. In itself, this output could be considered almost unbelievable, but then you have to add to the statistics the fact that the music in those seven years changed beyond all recognition and transformed rock music forever. Looking back, if you were not there, it really is hard to come to terms with. The sheer energy and busyness of their creative schedule over this time caused them to grow from a long haired boy band who appealed to the fellas as well, and sang, *she loves you yeah, yeah yeah*, to becoming artists and modern day poets who delved into the very fabric of the universe politically, socially, and spiritually, as well as writing the most crafted love songs of the century. And of course, as they traveled to new destinations in their artform, they were the ones, maybe along with Bob Dylan, who laid the tracks on which they traveled.

Harrison was the pretty face in the shadow of the genius of Lennon and McCartney, but from those shadows the younger member of the team quietly inspired and influenced much of what fired the story. A more thoughtful retrospective would alert you to the fact that he was the first to take The Beatles into the political realms, and did it with a reasonable dollop of humor in "Taxman" from *Revolver*. He was the one whom Bob Dylan connected with the best, hanging out with him in Woodstock in early 1970, jamming with him in a studio at the same time, and co-writing "I'd Have You All This Time," which appeared on Harrison's album, *All Things Must Pass*. He introduced the twelve string Rickenbacker to the new sounds of the '60s, first playing it on *A Hard Day's Night* and inspiring The Byrds to make it into a distinctive West Coast sound. Indeed, Harrison's sound should never be minimized in The Beatles' records. It was his distinctive guitar style that allowed the entire world to recognize their songs from the opening riffs. On the day after his death, Bob Geldof would say on BBC Radio 4, "I doubt there's a person listening to this show that can't remember each one of his guitar lines. Almost uniquely everything he played was a hook line."[1] On a Beatles' song before you got to the voice of Lennon or McCartney, Harrison had already given the song its signature.

It was he who, years before world music would become trendy, brought the Indian sitar into Western pop, playing it badly from all accounts on Norwegian Wood and continuing to experiment with it. The late '60s saw it on the cover of The Rolling Stones' *Their Satanic Majesties' Request* album and appearing in all kinds of places where it would have been unthinkable if a Beatle hadn't given it credence. There are blurs around the exact moment of Harrison's spiritual conversion, but it was a sitar and not a revival meeting that led him into his spiritual journey. Without doubt, though, it was a throw away scene from the *Help!* movie that set the domino effect in motion. A sitar played in an Indian restaurant caught Harrison's imagination both musically and spiritually. It is hard to say whether it was hindsight or not, but Harrison claimed that the music was a reawakening in him, that he had heard it before, that in some way he was hearing his native tunes. He suspected reincarnation, and it could be said that for a Westerner to find the drone of the sitar so beautiful might have the most skeptical atheist believing!

In the middle of the revolution with flowers in the bayonet, one man who had been at the very center of the war zone stopped to think. It is hard to tell at exactly what point George Harrison found Beatlemania an encroachment. In the closest thing we get to an autobiography, *I Me Mine*, he simply ignores the majority of the '60s, but somewhere Harrison stopped, and though he would not get off the music treadmill for a few more years, he started to change perspective. Being in the band that most symbolizes the time, indeed they were almost the history of the time incarnate, he was in maybe the best position to dissect the illusion that the hedonistic, existentialist, God-free party was not quite enough. If this was what the new youth idealized as what life was all about, Harrison was one who had everything they dreamed of and found no meaning. He would say, "Just certain things happened in my life which left me thinking 'What's it all about Alfie' and I remembered Jesus saying somewhere 'Knock and the door shall be opened' and I said (knock, knock) helloooo ... From the Hindu point of view each soul is potentially divine, the goal is to manifest divinity."[2]

And so Harrison brought God into the '60s. Whereas the British equivalent of Elvis, Cliff Richard's conversion to evangelical Christianity was of little consequence considering

Richard's new role as TV show host and Eurovision competitor (Eurovision is an annual inane songwriting competition), Harrison led The Beatles to the foothills of the Himalayas and the feet of the Maharishi Yogi, whose portly figure clad in white robes and graying Santa Claus beard make him one of the pictorial symbols of the summer of love. A working class Merseyside Catholic brought Eastern religion to the Western world. It is a huge statement, but hardly one that can be exaggerated. Whatever The Beatles did from long hair to drugs to wide multicolored ties, the world followed. When in interviews as late as 2001 Harrison would claim that half of the Hari Krishnas joined through his first solo number one, "My Sweet Lord," it would be hard to argue. The Beatles made Krishna cool.

A question that needs to be asked is why Harrison felt he needed to go Eastern. Why did the Jesus of his upbringing not meet the need to go beyond the material? Maybe his mate John Lennon hinted at the weakness in Jesus' street credibility when he made that famous statement to Maureen Cleave that The Beatles were bigger than Jesus. Though many Christians would get uppity and see it as some blasphemy, attending Beatles albums burning parties all over America, the truth is that Lennon was just telling the truth! How could four longhaired pop stars from Liverpool be more relevant to the world than someone who came to bring life in all its fullness? C.S. Lewis says that you only reject the God you are offered. It was not so much a rejection of Jesus that Harrison made, but an acceptance of Eastern philosophical thought in his attempt to transcend the material world.

Though Hinduism and Krishna are the religions that come to mind when you think George Harrison, the truth is that he was far from an orthodox believer of any one faith. Yes, his early days were spent supporting financially and with buildings the Hare Krishna movement, and he did produce an album of chants for the Radha Krishna Temple, but his spiritual influences widened as his journey continued. On the hymnal "Life Itself," he lists Christ, Vsnu, Buddha, Jehovah, Govindam, and Bismillah and sees them all as One Lord Creator of All. His wife Olivia would write after his death, "Though he often quoted spiritual greats in this way, George did not, contrary to popular belief, 'belong' to any spiritual organization, although many claimed him as their own."[3] She goes on to perhaps express an accurate assessment of her husband's beliefs, "Still, he managed to dive deep to the heart of each practice, never content to skim the surface. He embraced the essence of all religions although he had little patience for organized religions or dogma that espoused guilt, sin, or mystery."[4]

Harrison had often spoken with much suspicion on his Roman Catholic roots. In "Awaiting On You All," the vitriol against the Pope for owning shares in General Motors and knowing more about The Stock Exchange than God was such that EMI never printed it on the lyric sheet. Thirty years later in *Vatican Blues 2* where he describes himself as an ex-Catholic, he seems to have dismissed suspiciously the "Our Fathers" and "Hail Marys" as a little bit empty. Way back in 1968, Harrison would talk about the need for his faith to be real and not just a ritual. His quest was for a living dynamic of faith and not just thoughts, ideas, or rules and tradition—"if there's a God we must see Him, if there's a soul we must perceive it. Otherwise it is better not to believe. It is better to be an outspoken atheist than a hypocrite."[5] When asked why he added specifically Hare Krishna to the hallelujahs of "My Sweet Lord," he answered, "first of all hallelujah is a joyous expression that Christian have, but 'Hare Krishna' has a mystical side to it. It's more than glorifying God; it's asking to become His servant ... it's much closer to God than the Christianity is currently representing Him ... I think many teachers today are misrepresenting Christ. They're supposed to be representing Jesus but they are not doing it very well. They're letting Him down very badly, and that's a big turn off."[6] Most likely the traditional nature of his family's church-going in Liverpool had seemed empty and irrelevant to Harrison, but discovering through his music this vibrant mix of chanting and meditation was exactly the escape he needed from the madness of his Beatlemania. It was the chanting of GOD, GOD, GOD high above the temporal landscape that saw Harrison as some John The Baptist crying in the wilderness of "Bullsh– Avenue."

"Bullsh– Avenue" is how Harrison had always seen the world that he had experienced so intoxicatingly as a Beatle. His entire career is riddled with broadsides at a world that he saw as phony and sick and that will ultimately curtail your soul from finding its meaning and eternal peace. His songs have blatant attacks on the behavior of governments and industry and technology and the stock exchange. It was not the injustice or damage to the environment or invaded countries that is Harrison's biggest concern, though he pioneered charity concerts with his Bangladesh concert and triple album and joined Greenpeace in the '80s, but the damage to the individual soul that really distressed him. The material world and everything in it needed caring for, but the soul and eternity were even more important. In the personal testimony of "That Which I Have Lost" from his *Somewhere In England* record, humankind is losing a battle against dark forces whose falsehood will close the door to the sought after higher ground."

Harrison's answer to the world that weighs your spirit down is in meditation and mainly chanting. Harrison once boasted with a spiritual satisfaction that he traveled all the way from France to Portugal for twenty-three hours, chanting nonstop the entire way. He also claimed that one of the highlights of his life was helping the Radha Krishna Temple onto *Top Of The Pops*; he produced their album and released it on the Apple label. "Awaiting On You All" is a marvelous song and is up-front evangelistic about how it doesn't matter who you are or where you are from or what you have done because if you chant God's name enough you will find freedom. In his autobiography, *I Me Mine*, he writes that the song "is about Japa Yoga meditation which is repetition on beads (mala) of mantras. A mantra is mystical energy encased in a sound structure, and each mantra contains within its vibrations a certain power."[7]

The epitome song, "Living In The Material World," is another spiritual sermon/testimony, deep in spirituality, but full of biographical humor about The Beatles. This would be another of Harrison's traits. He inserts a lot of specific people and places and events in his lyrics, and he also has a habit of mixing the serious and frivolous together. The escape from the material world and his salvation in this song is through the grace of the Lord Sri Krishna. In *I Me Mine,* he would add commentary, "No matter how good you are you still need 'grace' to get out. You can be a yogi or a monk or a nun but without God's grace you still can't make it."[8]

This is orthodox evangelical Christianity. Not through Sri Krishna, of course, but through what Christ has done on the cross, and by His resurrection God offers His grace, unmerited favor, and Christians believe that is our only way out, our only means of salvation. Paul, in his letter to the Church in Ephesus, said, "For it is by grace you have been saved through faith, and this not from yourselves, it is a gift of God—not by works so that no one can boast."[9] In an interview on a Krishna website, Harrison adds another comment that seems to be a contradiction, "It's flexible. I think in one way I'm never getting out of here unless it's by His grace but then again, His grace is relative to the amount of desire I can manifest in myself. The amount of grace I would expect from God should be equal to the amount of grace I can gather or earn. I get out what I put in. Like in the song I wrote about Prabhupada, 'The Lord loves the ones that love the Lord ...'"[10] Harrison's definition of grace is certainly different than the evangelical Christian one.

Harrison's ultimate belief for salvation is in a reincarnation cycle. In the CD booklet for *Brainwashed*, there is a quote of Krishna to Arjuna in the Bhagavad-Gita: *There never was a time when you or I did not exist/ Nor will there be any future when we shall cease to be.* It is probably the most consistent theological concept throughout his records. The soul in this Hindu thought is eternal so to mention just two songs on the subject, he tells us on "Any Road" that it had no beginning and will never die and on *Gone Troppo*'s "Circles," he even uses the word "reincarnates" and tells us that we just go round and round.

When asked about where John Lennon's soul was now, Harrison answered, "I should hope that he's in a good place. He had the understanding, though, that each soul reincarnates until it becomes completely pure, and that each soul finds its own level, designated by reactions to its actions in this and previous lives."[11] His explanation in *I Me Mine* is, "When you're born, your life (past karma) is like a piece of string with knots in it and you've got to try, before you die, to undo all the knots: but you tie another twenty trying to get one undone."[12]

With the need in the cycle to purify your soul, Harrison has all kinds of songs of worship and prayer. Harrison's growing reputation and his moving out from under Lennon and McCartney's shadow was complete when he released *All Things Must Pass* a year after the band broke up. After being limited to a couple of songs an album, the breakup was like a laxative, and from the inner bowels of Harrison's songwriting ability poured out an album of ambitious scope. Produced by Phil Spector, it beats McCartney's *Band On The Run* and Lennon's *Imagine* as the best Beatles solo album. It also contained every aspect of Harrison's religious concerns. There was obviously the worship in his crossing of gospel and Krishna in the phenomenally successful single, "My Sweet Lord." "Hear Me Lord" is a prayer of open confession and honest spiritual pleading. The evangelist comes through in revivalist intensity in the aforementioned "Awaiting On You All" and devotional advice in "The Art Of Dying" and "Beware Of Darkness." Harrison's future albums would all touch on some of these disciplines, his music probably more consistent in its religious concern than it was in musical quality.

There is a little twist in the tail of Harrison's relationship with Christianity on the cover artwork of that posthumous *Brainwashed* album. For thirty years, his fans have been used to the OM sign appearing at various points on his album covers. There is no surprise to see it there again in the bottom right hand corner. But look again, and that is not a scuff alongside it. No, it is a cross. Why? This cannot have been a casual throwaway stroke of the pencil. Perhaps it is a significant indicator of how wide Harrison had thrown his spiritual search in the years before his death.

Of course he had never treated Jesus with anything other than the utmost respect; it was the Church that he had his issues with. Jesus gets mentions in a few songs, and on "Awaiting On You All," He is used as the name of God who one will see by the results of the salvation through one's chanting. In "I Me Mine," Harrison again gives a seemingly orthodox evangelical statement on Christ's cross. Speaking about "The Art Of Dying" and trying to explain the purging of karma for the purification of the soul at the end of the reincarnation cycle and of how when you reach that advanced level the gurus then take your karma on themselves, he says, "That is another reason for Christ's suffering. He took others' Karma in His own body as the 'Savior.'"[15] Change "karma" for "sin," and this then becomes a very orthodox belief in Christ's crucifixion.

Yet, why the cross that is solely the symbol of Christ's death

should now reappear as a Harrison symbol is fascinating. As
I prepared this chapter, my local paper ran a religious article
in which Belfast preacher Derrick Bingham relates the story
world traveling Christian evangelist Luis Palau told him about
a friend of his giving Harrison Christian literature at a Formula
One Grand Prix event. Harrison seemed to appreciate the
gesture and having read it. Palau's friend speaks of leading
Harrison to Jesus. If the cross is a clue to Harrison's new
understanding of Christianity, then the closing moments of
Brainwashed with a reading from *The Yoga Aphorisms of
Patanjali* and a traditionally Harrison chant of Hares declares
that he did not reject the one if there was a new acceptance of
the other. It throws up another question for those of us who
believe in Christ as the only way to God. Is the one belief that
Jesus is the way to God negated if you hold alongside it some
of the beliefs of other religions?

It was midmorning, and I had been having a lazy Easter
holiday with my family at our north coast cottage. The day
before, I had used my time to read and listen and immerse
myself in the music of George Harrison. I was making a bite
of lunch when onto the radio came Harrison's single "Any
Road." My mind flipped back into the analysis mode of the
previous night, and I found myself thinking how wonderful
it was that such a positive spiritual challenge was going out
over the airwaves. I was thinking about so many people out
in radio land who had no idea where they were going. They
needed to be challenged about the direction of their lives;
if the road they were on was heading anywhere. Preach it,
George, preach it! It was in disbelief that as the song faded
out, the presenter and his sidekick went on at some length
as to how they liked the song but what on earth was George
going on about! They were totally confused, saying it was
deep but very shallow.

Perhaps I was too tuned in by my day or two of wall to wall
Harrison, or maybe it was a sign of how prophetic a question

Harrison was asking. Had the world stopped asking one of humanity's most necessary questions. Where are we going? Harrison had been asking the question for almost forty years before he sadly passed away on November 30, 2001. The newspapers were filled with Harrison quotes for days, and the most common were, "Everything else can wait but the search for God ... " and that "the purpose of life is to find out, who I am. Why am I here? Where am I going?" If you listened really closely, you could hear the rock cry out the questions that this and every other generation needs to ask.

FIVE

NO ALARMS, NO SURPRISES PLEASE

I was on retreat with my students. That sounds grand, and you might ask what particularly beautiful place in Ireland we had chosen to reflect on higher things. Actually we were on a focused weekend in the very Hall of Residence where we live! On the Saturday night, we watched *Shawshank Redemption*. It is my favorite movie. My wife would tell you that I never remember movies. We have been known to watch some movies four or five times, and I still have no recollection of what happens. *Shawshank Redemption* is different. I have watched it so many times that I have almost memorized it. Having said that, recently I was saying how we never actually know whether the hero is innocent or not, and my students looked at me in disbelief! Watching it this time in the midst of a retreat type scenario gave the entire story a whole new significance.

The brutality, the injustice, and the everyday routine of prison life made a big impression on me this time. Then in the midst of all this, there were great moments of grace. I love that scene where our hero Andy gets all his mates a cold beer on the roof of the prison. Then there is that time when he finds the LPs and locks himself in the office so he can play an opera over the loud speaker to everyone in the prison yard, and the prisoners have a second or two of freedom because the music lifted them to transcendence. To use the cliché, life can be like that. It's hard. It's tough. But there are moments of grace that are like rumors or inklings of something more.

There is also that scene where Brooks doesn't want to leave the prison that he has been in for fifty years of his life. It reminded me of the man that Jesus asked if he really wanted to be healed. Healing for that man would be a ruination of his way of life. The only life he had ever known. Very much like the children of Israel in Egypt. There is a conditioned security in captivity. There is a fear of the unknown that freedom brings. Brooks couldn't hack it and commits suicide. Red describes it well. "At first you hate these walls, then you accept them, and eventually you become dependent on them."[1]

I thought about my students. Here they are, still in the relative innocence of the commercial, material world. They still have their parents paying the bills and the mortgage. They think with a youthful idealism that they will not get hooked into all of that. We had considered over the weekend the parable that Jesus told about the farmer sowing seeds. Some of the seed fell among the thorns and had a good root, but the things of the world, like money and fun, came and strangled it. I fear for my students, that at first they will hate the rat race, then they will accept it, and then they will learn to depend on it.[2]

Radiohead are the loudest of soul sirens when the walls are becoming comfortable or, God forbid, something that we are coming to depend on. They are a flashing light blinding us back from becoming simply those who want *no alarms and no surprises please*. And the alarm shudders and swirls and distorts and screams in a hopeless attempt to warn us of the blandness and meaninglessness of life in the twenty-first century. What thrilled me to bits was that I had this paragraph already written before their sixth album, *Hail To The Thief,* came out agreeing with me: *Your alarm bells should be ringing,* they tell us in "The Gloaming."

In a May 2003 interview with John Robinson for *NME*, Thom York stated his belief about the despair, "I sound like a loony, but there's an awful lot of shadows and malignant forces that are pulling strings at the moment. It's barely human, it's something that's coming from somewhere else, and it is impossible to control."[3] Yorke seems to be putting a dark transcendent evil being into the dock to take the blame for the mayhem of the late twentieth and early twenty-first century malaise that Radiohead have spent their careers shouting about. This being seems to be after our humanity, determined to tire it out, make it extinct, or on the verge of extinction at least. Yorke goes on, "Now I don't know if you have experienced this in your job, but in my job you meet people who have ceased to be human. You know how in an office there's always one person who's like this ambitious arsehole who doesn't care who he treads on, they actually think they are doing the right thing? Or if you meet a powerful politician—it's like shaking hands with thin air. The tornado has nothing in the middle. The gloaming to me is exploring this unhealthy darkness, which it seems it's impossible to counteract."[4]

The Gloaming is the subtitle of *Hail To The Thief*, and as Yorke puts it, describes not only their most recent ruminations, but the spiritual space that the band has inhabited all along. On the surface they have looked at a vast range of issues, from technology and work to modern transport to commerce,

advertising and globalization to pretty suburban avenues
to third world debt and the African AIDS pandemic to
government and a few wars fought here and there in the last
few years. Some of these more than others are clearly seen
as the works of that dark demeanored ethereal presence, but
some would hardly be called demonic; indeed, they would
be seen as good, and yet even the less threatening are all
involved in the conspiracy to dehumanize.

If the devil arrived at my student retreat, what do you
reckon his tactics would be? Would he throw them a gun to
kill their neighbor, a condom and $100 for the prostitute he
had ordered for them, or a syringe with enough heroine to
trap them in addiction overnight? Acutely aware that their
reasoning for being at the retreat in the first place would make
this group a little harder to penetrate, evil's subtle despot
would be likely to seek out a more effective strategy, like
lulling them into a false sense that they were free from such
dangerous onslaughts and then sucking the vitality from their
spirits by placing them on a treadmill that looks good and
tastes good and has them being respected as good from all
who would come to know and work with them.

"No Surprises" is perhaps the most accessible of Radiohead's
songs. It is almost the prettiest sheen of a pop song with that
tenderly beautiful guitar and glockenspiel. Like the entire
album, *OK Computer*, it is concerned with the busy and
comfortable third millennium human with a heart that is as
full of waste as a landfill and who is happy to settle for the
quiet life, the poisonous fumes and a life of *no alarms and
no surprises please*. In the end a pretty house and a pretty
garden and no alarms or surprises is the desire of the day. It
is an option on the menu of adulthood. To be truthful it is not
a decision to make, but like our protagonists in *Shawshank
Redemption* and my students as they make a last step into
adulthood, it is a sentence that we are handed unawares,
hating the walls, getting used to them as if this is the only way

it can be, and finally becoming resigned and finding security in our captivity. Unawares, we could be heading right into the "jaws of hell" as they describe it unaware on "Sit Down, Stand Up."

Cornel West is a black American political thinker who leans heavily on "Christian pragmatism and Marxist analysis." In his provocative contribution to American life, he took umbrage at Bill Clinton's feely weelyness of the good times of the '90s, suggesting that "America is a hotel civilization ... obsessed with comfort and convenience and contentment."[5] A nation is ignoring its pain and the reality of the world to live away from the streets in a place where there are no alarms and no surprises. In her analysis of West's thought in her book, *Cornel West: The Politics of Redemption*, Rosemary Cowan said what West that what realized America needs are "truth tellers ... who will force difficult issues into the American consciousness and force the nation to confront pain."[6] West knows more about blues and jazz—and maybe more surprising for a man of his vintage gangster rap than he does about Radiohead, but Radiohead are doing exactly what he states is needed. *Kid A* and *Amnesiac* were albums that jolted the conscience and forced confrontation. The sound and the feeling were as strong a weapon as the words and their meaning.

Radiohead might be seen as an English counterpart to the Irish U2. Bono and Thom York are two frontmen who have worked together campaigning in the Jubilee 2000 Campaign for the cancellation of world debt. For both of them, the primary concern in their work is the soul. Where they diverge is their respective geographical locations that give their songs very different slants. Whereas U2 emerged out of a God-drenched Irish society, some of that good and some of that bad, Radiohead are hewn from an English post-Christian society. This would result in U2 being flag waving message bringers, always hoping, ever believing and determined to proclaim their truth. Radiohead on the other hand have never been around belief, at least of the transcendent kind. They are therefore not so much in the business of sending out messages for transformation as they are in simply telling us how it is and warning us of the state that we are in and the tragedy we are hurtling toward.

In a discussion with *Q* magazine's Phil Sutcliffe about an "against demons" hex that went underneath the *OK Computer* CD, Yorke blurs his meaning, "The 'against demons' idea is not believing in God or the devil, it's just that act of drawing a hex on a door to protect yourself."[7] It sounds a lot like an English secularist bereft of the resources to believe in what you believe. Ireland's forty shades of fertile green fields of religion on the other hand allow Bono to wear his faith on his sleeve without reservation.

It does make life tricky when the spiritual is your obsession and its survival your life's work, yet there is no belief in God, the spirit in the word spiritual. It is the soul that Radiohead are campaigning for because they see it as an endangered species. They suggest that if we all stand together and *immerse our souls in love* ("Street Spirit (Fade Out)") we can turn around the state of the world and prevent the sucking of the blood of the young. This is not about campaigning for outward causes like rainforests and stopping wars and Tibetan injustice or Third World debt, even though all of those things have Radiohead's committed support. This is about the underneath, this is about the unseen, and this is about the inside. This is about the more important wars raging in our universe, as Paul wrote, "We put our trust not on what is seen because what is seen is temporary but on what is unseen because what is unseen is eternal."[8]

If "No Surprises" shows us the numb comfort of the hotel mind-set and *a job that slowly kills you*, then "Fake Plastic Trees" is about our slavery to the artificial in products, relationships, government, and entertainment. It comes on like a '90s version of John Lennon's "Nowhere Man," the thirty years in-between turning humanity into a fake, plastic, polystyrene commodity without a soul. Artificial is gravity dragging us down, and no one can fight the new rules of nature, so Yorke ends up "scared that there is nothing underneath." "Dollars and Cents" turns us into what we have ended up most desiring—money, in a variety of currencies! No wonder that in "Subterranean Homesick Alien," the visiting beings from outer space are fascinated by "weird creatures" stressed out and damaging their bodies to look and feel better.

In the end on "2 + 2 = 5" from *Hail to the Thief,* they are convinced that it is the devil having his way with us and that we are trapped by him because we have not been "paying attention." The title is an Orwellian reference to our believing the lies we are thrown. Our attention is what Radiohead are after. The head shaking rant is Yorke's frustrated attempts to make us think. Bertrand Russell would say, "Most people would die rather than think." Christian thinker and writer Os Guinness applies that thought wonderfully in his book, *The Gravedigger File*, in which he reveals the secret papers of the devil's plans to subvert the modern Church: "most Christians, as a current jibe runs, would die rather than think—in fact they do."[9] In the movie, *The Truman Show*, Jim Carey plays the part of a man, Truman Burbank, whose entire life has been conditioned in the world's largest television studio where all the people in his family and life are actors. The director of the soap opera extravaganza is asked why Truman has never caught on to the deception upon which his life is built. The director replies that "we accept the reality we are given."[10] Radiohead are adamant that they can shake us out of acquiescent acceptance of what the media injects into our soul stream as absolute truth, that causes our unconscious paralysis and demise.

Radiohead put their prophetic wake-up call into the music

61 | FIVE

and do not just shout their protests like some latter day Dylan.
Yorke speaks of hearing a cassette tape interview with John
Coltrane where he says he was once involved in politics but
he then decided to put it all into his horn as everywhere else
was ugly. Radiohead do something similar. Lyrically they can
be obscure and obtuse, and in interviews they skirt around
issues, denying and confusing as much as they ever spell out
their intentions. Where Dylan's railing against societal ills
was to the backdrop of an acoustic guitar, the words being
all important, Radiohead are for the postmodern subjective
right side of the brain. For someone born on the very edges
of the Generation X culture, it took me a little while to grasp
not only the sound but more importantly the message. From
my traditional conditioning, I began asking why the song was
not enough and why artists like Elliott Smith and Badly Drawn
Boy had to fill up all their work with noises and loops and
samples and clutter. This of course is a postmodern approach
to music, painting shades and moods and feelings with
atmosphere and beautiful sounds as much as with the words.

There world is divided in two. There are those who
remember the very first television that came into their homes.
Then there are those who do not and who have lived with a
television in the living room, the basement, the bedrooms,
the kitchen and have had to fight to keep it out of the
washroom! As I pointed out in *Walk On: The Spiritual Journey
of U2*, this creates very different ways of learning. Those who
remember the first television arriving will have learned in
linear fashion and sieve information through the objective
side of their brain. Those who have always had a relationship
with the colorful and noisy family friend in the corner of
the room will have been taught in an image dominated
environment and will have used the subjective side. Think
of that advertisement on the TV that has no words and never
mentions the product. The "right-siders" cannot even imagine
how the "left-siders" are not getting the message.

Iceland's Sigor Ros have perhaps taken it to the nth degree with their album ( ). On the album packaging, there are no words at all, no title, no credits, no lyrics—nothing! Then the lyrics themselves have been sung so that the listener can hear whatever the listener hears, rather than what the singer is trying to say. It is a bizarre, but fascinating, pioneering if you will—even a hardliner like myself has come to realize. It would be easy to dismiss these sounds as an emperor parading around naked as a jaybird but you do so at your own peril and emotional subjective loss.

This is particularly true of Radiohead. Dismiss *Kid A* as some experimental distraction while they wait to make another *OK Computer,* and you miss the point completely. I wonder if it would be the most self-indulgent thing I have ever done to quote myself? Here is what I wrote about Radiohead's warm-up gig before the *OK Computer* tour in the tiny Mandela Hall in the Students Union of the university where I am Presbyterian chaplain. "It was a bit like a private party as just over 500 fans were spellbound and in disbelief as this exceptional band played a warm-up gig for their RDS show on Saturday. The hype is high after Monday's release of the far from difficult third album *OK Computer* and the new songs mingled with the more immediate favorites from 'The Bends' and of course 'Creep.' Guitars shimmered, swirled, and swathed and then went burning, blistering and bludgeoning behind Thom York's unique vocal. This boy is one minute angel and next the *X-Files* freak of the week. The gig too is one massive contrast, stop and start, gentleness and frenzy, beauty and terror, tenderness and rage, hope and despair. Quite indescribable and like nothing else the world of Britpop has to offer. Phil Spector never imagined a wall of sound like 1997. 'Airbag' and 'Paranoid Android' take more time to seep through than 'Fake Plastic Trees,' 'Street Spirit' or 'High and Dry,' yet 'Lucky' and 'The Tourist' are personal favorites tonight, but this band are going to be around for long enough to give you time. They are probably by now the best rock

band in the world and last night they played in Queens'
Students Union. Nice dream."[10]

As you can tell, I was a believer! When *Kid A* was released,
I read with a little concern the reviews, and though my
friend Geoff warned me not to purchase, how could I not!
The consternation was immediate, and the backsliding
lasted for years. Then—revival! Maybe it was the perpetual
bombardment of my friend David Dark's faithful witness,
either in private or in public seminar. He would always have
me on the verge of seeing the point of these guys who had
made guitars shine, leave them down to push plugs into
boards, and pull them out again!

The distorted and grating awkwardness of the quantum leap
between *OK Computer*'s gentle closing trilogy and everything
seemingly being in the wrong place in *Kid A*'s opening song
so fittingly or unfittingly titled "Everything In The Right Place"
is the entire point of Radiohead's prophetic memorandum.
Never the hypocrites, the Oxford band followed the success
of *OK Computer*, that put them close to the "best band on the
planet" label, by setting off the loudest alarms and turning
surprise to shock, as they released an album of musically
disjointed impressionistic avant garde that would in its very
existence ask questions of the pop world's attitude to product
and charts and fame and art.

The question to ask is, when Radiohead's sirens swirl and
sound and get your soul's attention, can they guide you
toward an escape exit? Are they like Andy in *Shawshank
Redemption,* chipping away at the walls that many get to
depend on in order to break out beyond them into a new
day of hopes and dreams and painting boats down the deep
blue sea and sky of a Mexican coastal paradise? David Fricke
in his *Hail To The Thief* interview with Thom Yorke writes,
"Yorke insists that despite the album's black air of politics
and paranoia, *Hail to The Thief* is not a soundtrack for digging

bunkers. The album's dark rhythms and fighting guitars are the surge and clang of engagement, not escape."[12]

The birth of Yorke's son seems to have given him some new hope. Like all births, new little humans come with an acute awareness of possibilities and potential, not yet tarnished or spoiled by the blood suckers that occupy the vast majority of Radiohead grooves. A new baby to pull him "out of the air crash" ("Lucky") has given him time to think more of the future than just recriminating the past or warning against the present. Intriguingly named Noah, he again follows Bono's trait of Biblical names for his children. Yet Bono's biblical names Eve, Jordan, Elijah, and Abraham John do not have the same ring of meaning as Noah, the man who saw the world in "the gloaming" of his day, souls cracked and lost, and with transcendent insight, built his own escape.

Hail To The Thief has obvious child-in-the-house references, with genies coming out of bottles, monsters, dinosaurs, and even a play on the children's story "Chicken Licken," where a fox lures the cuddly animals into a shed to tear them limb from limb while they try to tell the king that the sky is falling. In *Q*, Yorke says, "I love that idea of there being no intention of a happy ending,"[13] which might tell us something about the inherent joy in the gloom and doom pronouncements of Radiohead. He goes on though to expound the text of the story with a profound and contemporary application, "and the worst thing is that they don't get to tell the king that the sky is falling in … That could be happening everyday of our lives. The ones with the news are getting knocked on the head."[14]

With the album title's nod to the most laughed at (outside the U.S.A.!) election results in history that brought George W. Bush to power and set us on the road to war in Iraq, Yorke, while characteristically smudging the Bush connection, also sees that election week as a defining moment in the album's content. "It was a formative moment—one evening on the radio, way before we were doing the record, the BBC was running stories about how the Florida vote had been rigged and how Bush was being called a thief. That line threw a switch in my head. I couldn't get away from it. And the light—I was driving that evening with the radio on—was particularly weird. I had this tremendous feeling of foreboding, quite indescribable, really. To me, all the feelings on the record stem from that moment."[15] The bopped on the head farm animals might therefore be the Steve Earles, Dixie Chicks, Michael Moores, et al, who warned us that the sky was in a precarious condition.

Yorke, however, does not want Noah bumped on the head. He is determined that he "won't let it happen to my children." There is a new defiance to the inclinations of the age. Change from somewhere is vital. He dreams and wishes and who knows prays in his Radiohead kind of way that Noah might turn it around. There is another veiled swipe at Bush on "Sail To The Moon" when he surmises that maybe his son could end up President but hopes he would "know right from wrong," before Noah takes on the messianic role of his Old Testament namesake and builds an ark in the flood to sail us to the moon.

Moments of light do exist in Radiohead's muse, but they are as few and very far between as color in the first three quarters of *Shawshank Redemption*. There are born again moments and salvation by an airbag or through aliens lifting them from outside themselves to salvation and a new sense of meaning and perspective. In his book about the re-definition of apocalypse, David Dark suggests, "We do well to view Radiohead's work as an advocate in all efforts at increased understanding, redemptive response and discerning engagement of this wide-open world."[16] That is their prophetic edge. Like the parents heading home and making every effort to keep their children awake, they jerk us out of complacent comfort and have us wide-eyed with near frightened alertness as they swerve all over the road with the radio turned up to near unbearable volumes. They wake us up; they refuse to allow us to drift back into sleep. They are adamantly refusing to just succumb. They are going to fight for the survival of the soul and thus humanity's most defining attribute. They still hate the walls and will do whatever it takes to never allow my students to get used to them, or worse still, dependent on them. Once they have our attention, there may be uncertainty about how they are going to turn the tide around, but maybe that is for someone else. Maybe even Noah Yorke? Maybe my students? Maybe me?

WE'VE GOT TO GET OURSELVES BACK TO THE GARDEN

I t is the hottest of Canadian afternoons. As the guests gather for a wedding on the water's edge of the Lake Of Bays, I am aware of the shadow cast by the boat house that will give the guests some relief from the heat. The shadow misses where I will stand with the bride and groom. It is the first wedding a scruffy cleric like myself will have to think about what to wear; will my sunblock be SPF 20 or 30?! I am even more acutely aware of the beauty of this place. For twenty-four hours we have partied and celebrated and enjoyed the refreshment of the water. The trees are just pre-fall green; the lake glistens, and a few motor boats cut across its surface.

Not so much distracted by the surroundings as inspired by them, I think about what to say to Ewan and Miriam as they set out from this prettiest of places and head down the aisle made between their family and friends to begin a new life together. They are activists. Their friends who have gathered literally from all over the world are activists. There are those working with AIDS charities, development charities, and human rights campaigns, as well as those who work or volunteer with the mentally and physically challenged. Not all would claim that they do it for any Christian motivation. Some would reject the very idea of God, but others would have had Christian faith as an influence in their formative years even if they are unsure of where Jesus fits into their worldview now or they into His.

Add to all this the parents and friends all being from very different geographical and spiritual homes, and the preacher's job is never an easy one. There is a lead though. Ewan and Miriam have a thing with songs about gardens, and the two songs in their minds as they prepared invitations and all that wedding paraphernalia were Van Morrison's "In The Garden" and Joni Mitchell's "Woodstock." A Belfast man where I am from and a Canadian woman where I was now preparing. The more I considered and pondered, the more sure I was that the text for the service should be from the canon of Canada's finest songwriter: *We are stardust, we are golden/ And we've got to get ourselves back to the garden.* Perfect!

When Joni Mitchell wrote those words, the hippy children of the '60s thought they were and believed they could be! The gates of Eden had never looked so close. If you examine the fingernails of the '60s hippy children, you might find traces of the gold of heaven's streets where they touched it and then were mercilessly dragged away again. Whatever led to it, Woodstock was the pinnacle of the hippy dream. It was the highest point, and the falling back down was quick and painful.

Rock music had been the catalyst. The entire play was acted

out on the stage of pop and rock. The Beatles and Bob Dylan had opened doors, and drugs had fueled the journey. By the summer of love in 1967, Eastern religion had given a spiritual dimension, and the free love peace train and the uninhibited sex that came with it reached Woodstock on a weekend in August 1969.

Joni Mitchell was not at the festival, held back from going in order to appear on television on the Monday night. Yet, it was her who encapsulated the moment and the era in the song that would weave its way onto the soundtrack of the movie sung by Crosby Stills and Nash. Returning from the biggest festival in rock history, Stephen Stills—the middle name in that super group—had been trying to write a song of his experience of the day but his ideas were made redundant when Mitchell pulled up a chair and played maybe her most poetic and prophetic song. It is a song for the specific that can be rendered useful in the universal. It is a song that can be sung at any gathering where people meet with any kind of hope about the present and future. It was written about one event of the '60s, but could be seen as the definitive commentary on the entire hippy movement. It not only captures that moment in time, but it lives beyond the event or the era. It is a song about humankind, about who humankind is and what humankind should be setting out to achieve.

Within three verses Mitchell deals with the resentments of that hippy people. There is the smog. There is the alienation of being just a cog that spins around and around monotonously. There is the anti-war dream of bombers turning into butterflies. It is about getting back to the land. Then there is the spiritual dimension. In *Goldmine* magazine in 1995, Mitchell revealed that she was going through quite a spiritual experience at the time. "At the time I was going through a kind of born again Christian trip, not that I went to any church, I'd given up on Christianity at an early age at Sunday School. But suddenly, as performers we were in a position of having so many people look to us for leadership, and for some unknown reason I took it seriously and decided I needed a guide and leaned on God. So I was a little 'God-mad' at the time, for a lack of a better term, and had been saying to myself, 'Where are the modern miracles?' Woodstock, for some reason impressed upon me as being a modern miracle."[1] In the end she thought she had found eternal truth in this free love, naked kick against the values of the modern world. So the spiritual dimension is not coincidental. This is an attempt to get the soul free. There is the idea that we have all got into this mess by getting "caught up in the devil's bargain."

If you study her lyrics a little deeper from that time, it's easy to see things of a spiritual nature that are creeping into her poetry. On the most beautiful and accurate attack on the male sexual psyche, decades ahead of the Alanis Morrisettes, "Woman of Heart and Mind," she talks of holiness being the latest craze. Then there is "A Case Of You." Some of the sharper heads in music would suggest that if you have a weak track on an album, you should hide it away on side two and track four. On *Blue*, that is exactly where Mitchell places maybe her best song of all. And there again we hear references to "holy wine" and "touching souls."

All the best of human causes are about striving toward a better day of peace or community or justice or whatever, and Joni says, journeying forward is actually a journey back—to the Garden where it all began, where it was not like it is today. Can we not get back there again? The Judeao-Christian perspective on Eden is of God having a close connection with His creations, particularly the one made in His image— humanity. Human beings had a unique relationship with God; they were co-workers with Him in His world, and they had an inheritance of beauty and goodness to live within. This they squandered for a moment of pleasure and the desire to be God themselves. All relationships were fractured—with God, with the land, and with each other. Ever since mankind has lived east of Eden, living something less than the harmony originally intended. Woodstock was for Mitchell some kind of image of a restoration of the creation peacefulness.

In 1994, Mitchell wrote another song about the fulfilment of human history. Well, actually, she paraphrased Irish poet W.B. Yeats' vision of apocalypse. In his poem, "Second Coming," he sees not a return to the garden, but history's fate "slouching towards Bethlehem to be born." It is an intriguing link. Woodstock directs us back to where the Old Testament began, and "Slouching Towards Bethlehem" points to where the New Testament story of redemption entered the world in the form of Christ.

The two songs could not be more contrasting. Yeats is not hopeful of peace descending, but instead he sees a rising doom, the antichrist smashing to pieces the misguided illusion that humanity was evolving in some kind of enlightened way. Yeats wrote "Second Coming" in 1919. For two centuries humanity had believed in her progress. Science and technology was bringing man into a new day when the troubles of the world could be put to right. Then came the First World War. Man's inhumanity to man had never been so fierce. This was no sign of a better day. This was no clue to some twentieth century paradise.

For Mitchell to choose such a poem to adapt to her own art should not be a surprise. From Woodstock on, her work has not been so much about the Garden or how to get back to the garden, but about the hell we are living in outside of the garden. Stephen Holden for *The New York Times* recalls a story of a young man approaching a table that Sting, Bruce Springsteen, and Don Henley were sharing with Mitchell. As the young man went on about the '60s, she burst his bubble saying, "Don't be romantic about it—we failed."

"At least you tried," retorted the man.

"But we didn't try hard enough. We didn't learn from history. If any progress is to be made, we must show how we failed."[2]

When asked by Phil Sutcliffe in an interview for *Q* magazine whether she was aware of being the spokesperson for a generation she replied, "You mean via the song 'Woodstock?' If I was a spokesperson, nobody heard me, so big deal."[3]

In the '80s and '90s, Mitchell made sure she didn't fail in the exposing of the failure and her not being heard. *Dog Eat Dog* is Mitchell's harshest and most intensely political album. Produced by the weird whim of the day, electro pop boy Thomas Dolby, during his fifteen minutes of fame, it is a raging torrent of judgment on modern ills. As she spells out very clearly in "Fiction," these are songs about deluded dreams and the empty desires of hedonism that advertisers create for the rich big business empires. The imbalances of capitalism are a recurring theme on an album filled to overflowing with racketeers, big-wig financiers, thieves, and sycophants selling short-lived products, shiny toys, and even power and the justice system. On the title track, she gives her apocalyptic warning that every culture is on its last legs and that those who are taking any notice know that everything worthwhile will be thrown away.

On another song Mitchell names the powers, the three great stimulants, that have us cursed—avarice, brutality, and innocence. Avarice must point to the deceptive trickery of the men in suits who can sell snow to Eskimos; the brutality must be a hint at Reaganism in Central America, as well as violence on the streets and in the family home. How, you might ask, could innocence be a stimulant to a disintegrating culture? She explained to Iain Blair of the *Los Angeles Herald*, "Innocence has always been a stimulant especially when a culture is entering a decadent period. You get kiddie porn,

the cult of the youth, an obsession with youth in fact, and
stuff like face-lifts—yech!"[4]

Another power that is named and blamed on *Dog Eat Dog*
are the snakebite evangelists that get completely exposed
in "Tax Free." The rise in influence of the fundamentalist
conservative right wing churches was most clearly in
evidence from the television pulpits of the likes of Jerry
Falwell, Pat Robertson, and Jimmy Swaggert. Mitchell's
musical collaborator and husband of the time Larry Klein
told Joni biographer Kate O'Brien about watching Swaggert
on television. "We were amazed at the whole spectacle of this
thing, this guy who was claiming to represent Jesus Christ
and who was advocating all kinds of wild things, including
bombing Cuba."[5]

"Tax Free" is a powerful indictment of Swaggert and his kind.
Rod Steiger becomes the preacher from hell who recalls the
worn out theme of rock 'n' roll being of the devil, but then to
a much more sinister effect suggests attacking Cuba with a
surety of divine approval that Dylan had so ably challenged
in "God On Our Side" two decades before. Mitchell's problem
here is not only the marriage of church and state, particularly
in the right wing conservative nature of that marriage in the
USA, but her inability to understand the contradictions in
the preaching. The judgmentalism and seeming hate that
pervades the attitude with which the so-called love of Christ
is preached is no conduit for the Good News of the Gospel
to travel through to the soul. Politically, the contradiction is
similar in its dichotomy; how can they speak of a Prince of
Peace when there is war mongering militancy at work?

If her political commentary was in your face on *Dog Eat Dog*,
the albums that followed all touched on similar themes. Her
vehemence might have been a little more gently produced
and a little more scattered through the record, but they
probably stand out more as a result. On *Chalk Mark In The*

Rain, there is "Number 1," that again looks at the rat race and the need for success, and "The Beat Of Black Wings," again about violence, this time specifically about a paratrooper medic who served in Vietnam. "Lakota" is a poignant look at the theft of the native Indian land. Here again there is a link between injustice and those who came in the name of their white God to do it. She would later talk about how she was introduced to prejudice and bigotry by the treatment of her schoolmate Mary, an adopted American Indian girl about whom she wrote "Cherokee Louise" on *Night Ride Home*.

"Sex Kills," on the Grammy winning *Turbulent Indigo*, began on the last night of the L.A. riots when Joni pulled up behind a car with personal license plates. She introduced the song explaining, "this guy had the licence plate JUST ICE ... and I never really thought about that word quite in that manner ... justice JUST ICE ... so in the weeks that followed and especially in the uproar we were there ... I asked everybody I knew about justice, what is it ... everybody wants it, nobody knows what it is ... I even read Plato's *Republic* which was based on the premise if you build a just society you could have justice ... so Plato describes the Socratic just society but it would be unjust to the likes of me because it was a society of specialists. You had to be a painter, a poet, or a musician, but you couldn't tackle all three so I would already be pinched in this society so I don't know to this day what a just society, or what justice is but this is kind of what went down."

The song itself jam packs as much social commentary into less than four minutes as was on the entire *Dog Eat Dog* treatise. Underneath the recurring riff of "sex kills," there are dodgy doctors prescribing all kinds of pills, rapists, gun-toting children, and a world being rent asunder with oil spills and gas leaks. In the end, she asks if justice is at the mercy of the greedy and the lustful, and if the world is simply a place where the weak are sacrificed for the good of the strong. Again, we are a long way from the visions of "Woodstock."

Another song on *Turbulent Indigo*, "Magdalene Laundries,"
is the other side of the "Tax Free" coin. Across the world
geographically and spiritually, another Christian orthodoxy
shuns Mitchell's sense of believing. With a cheerier tune at
her disposal, Mitchell, it seems, picked up the *Toronto Star* at
the grocery store and read about an Irish scandal of how the
selling of a property of the Sisters Of Charity in north Dublin
unearthed 133 bodies of the "fallen women" who were sent to
convent laundries for sexual misdemeanors. With the bodies
the horror of the treatment of these young girls who might
have been prostitutes or unmarried mothers was uncovered,
the Roman Catholic Church had another scandal to deal with,
as well as the child abuse cases that would pour out over the
next decade. To give the song an Irish context, Mitchell first
recorded it with the Irish traditional band The Chieftains on
their 1999 release *Tears Of Stone*.

The song points out the same fundamental flaw "Tax
Free" did for the television evangelists. She is naming the
unbelievable hypocrisy of such a heartless place being
called Our Lady of Charity and a painful shrugged chortle
proceeds a repeat of the ironic "charity." That Mitchell is not
dismissing Jesus with the abhorrence carried out in His name
is evident as she suggests that if these people had any idea of
who Jesus was or what He was about, they would not be so
damning and cruel, but would drop their stones of judge and
jury just as Jesus told those religious leaders who had caught
a woman in adultery and were waiting for His verdict so that
they could stone her.

Years later a movie about the laundries, *Magdalene Sisters*,
would be released. In an interview with director Peter Mullan
for BBC Northern Ireland, Ralph McLean asked Mullan how
such things could have happened. Mullan had asked a nun
involved in the laundries the very same question, and she
answered "absence of doubt." For many believers doubt is
treated with suspicion, but the Sister had put her finger on

a great truth. When humans take the strength of their belief and ease it across the thin line to absolute knowledge, then arrogance can lead to all kinds of things being done in the name of God. Mystery is what saves us from such abuses as Mitchell is highlighting. As the apostle Paul reminds us in a chapter that Mitchell had used in her song "Love," "we see but through a glass darkly." The mistake of believing that we can see any clearer can have repugnant results. Nations can invade nations, churches can exclude those who do not think like them, and individuals can treat their neighbors in the most dismissive, judgmental, and damaging ways. A look back at "Slouching Towards Bethlehem" finds Mitchell summing it up as she concludes, sadly, that those who are good have no conviction, but even worse, those who have a passion lack the mercy to use it compassionately.

So has Joni Mitchell's repugnance with things carried out by the orthodox churches masquerading as being done in the name of God completely unraveled that conversion experience that she talked about three decades ago? Has she lost all faith and hope that her Christian obsession in the late '60s gave her? Not at all. Though Mitchell herself would never in any way articulate in terms of being a Christian, she has never given up on God. In a *Mojo* interview with Barney Hoskins in 1994, she talks about the difficult life she has had. It is easy to overlook a life that was struck down early by polio, that had to give up a daughter for adoption, and that experienced a miscarriage, as well as the usual romantic heartache. She is not looking for special attention. She says, "I have had a difficult life as most people have ... a life of very good luck and very bad luck ... but I don't think I've ever become faithless; I've never been an atheist, although I can't say what orthodoxy I belong to."[6]

"Woodstock"-like visions and dreams are far from lost in Mitchell's later work. "Passion Play" from the same album, *Night Ride Home*, that gave us "Slouching Towards

Bethlehem," is a song of Gospel story and Gospel truth. Mary
Magdalene is getting better press than she would an album
later in "Magdalene Laundries" and Zaccheus is almost at the
top of the tree of sinners (excuse the pun!). To those in need
come redemption and a heart healer, strays in the wilderness
now with someone who has met them in their wanderings.
The Messiah arrives into a world that is "divinely barren" but
"wickedly wise." In the extensive liner notes to *The Complete
Geffen Recordings*, she writes, "This song is basically my
telling of the Easter story but it morphs into contemporary
ecological and sociological disasters. It is about crisis in
the heart and healing of the heart."[7] She is looking for *Thy
kingdom come/ Thy will be done,* and in looking hard for the
kingdom, Mitchell is taking another look back to the Garden.
The kingdom that Jesus came to bring is a future day, but
it will take us back to our original intentions in that garden,
where we were stardust and golden.

In 2002, Mitchell released an intriguing record of orchestrated
covers of her own songs. Having produced an album of the
pre-rock 'n' roll classics two years previous, on which she
had dropped in her own "Both Sides Now" and "A Case Of
You," Mitchell took twenty-two songs that covered her entire
career and put them into the very same musical setting.
It was a revelation. Musical director Larry Klein brought
together an orchestra and jazz players and gave his ex-wife's
work new resonance and drama in the most tasteful and
subtle of ways. His ex-wife's voice gives the tunes a new
slant too, seemingly deeper than her Baez-like wail, probably
resulting somewhere between the abuse of cigarettes and the
wisdom of maturity.

The packaging is immaculate. Mitchell's paintings have
graced her work since the beginning, and portraits have
been very regular in recent releases, but inside the outer
box, there is a book between the CDs in the digipack where
we get an independent piece of Mitchell's art, her paintings

complimented by quotations from her songs. Getting the opportunity to read her visual images alongside her poetic ones is a highly intoxicating mix.

The booklet is all wrapped in quotes from "Love," "Slouching Towards Bethlehem," "Amelia," "The Circle Game," and a few other snippets of "Woodstock," along with "Refuge From The Roads," where the album gets its title. If the booklet gives a hint of the spiritual life still in Mitchell's palette, guitar case, heart, and soul, then the sequencing of the tracks on the CD itself offers up another little illumination. The center of the first CD sees "Love" followed by "Woodstock," neatly placed alongside the yang of their yin in "Slouching Towards Bethlehem." Two songs later we find "The Sire Of Sorrow (Job's Sad Song)" where Mitchell, in the alias of the Old Testament character Job, asks what he has done to deserve all that has befallen him. It is a lament of epic proportions, as indeed is the Old Testament book. But in some ways, it is the reality of our place between the Garden and the kingdom; justice is impossible to find, and yet it does not negate a faith in God, but asks questions of Him—and indeed us—in the meantime.

Back to that wedding. In the sweat-inducing temperatures of North Ontario, I got a little heated under the collar. It was not the infantile shouting from the loudest speedboat ever launched that cut rudely through the tranquillity of the place and the atmosphere of the romantic meeting the sacred. During my talk, for some reason, I was drawn to John Lennon's most famous secular hymn, "Imagine." Quoting, *Imagine there's no heaven,* I got a little wound up at the late great Beatle and raged that it was too easy to imagine that there is not a heaven. What I was going to do was more difficult. I was going to imagine that there was one, then have a vision of what it was like, and then go even further and attempt to bring that heaven down to earth. I wanted to commit to getting us back to the Garden. I invited our newlyweds and their family and friends to join me on that pilgrimage.

For Joni Mitchell, her vision of paradise was not the end of her journey. It was the beginning. Traveling west back toward Eden (interestingly the wise men in the Gospel account of Jesus birth came from the East), has been full of confrontation with the trials and tribulations of living outside the Garden. She is an artist without doubt disappointed that paradise was not as close in 1969 as she and so many others hoped it was. Her work is now filled with the reality of humanity's failure to achieve the prophetic dream of her song, but never without the hope that that day will come.

SEVEN

ALIVE IN THE WORLD

n 1996 on a sunny Belfast evening, I watched Jackson
Browne make his speeches between songs and in songs
during an open air concert in Botanic Gardens half a
mile away from my front door. It was very powerful
rhetoric, and my mind threw up a little suspicion. As he sang
about poverty and the marginalized and as he pricked my
conscience with his sharp needles of literate philosophy,
I suddenly started to question: What would he know? I do
not think it was the fact that my wife was bewitched by his
pretty Californian looks, hoping that I would look like that
when I was fifty, because I certainly did not look as good at
thirty-five! No. He is a pop star. He has an L.A. tan. He lives in
some Hollywood mansion. What would he know to be in any
position to preach at me? Then he sang "Alive In The World"
from his *Looking East* album, and right there, as if mind-
reading my judgments, he answered me loud and clear.

"Alive In The World" is Jackson Browne demanding of himself. It is a pop star in the Hollywood hills keeping himself in check. It is the wealthy successful activist making sure that that contradiction does not allow him to get lethargic and apathetic and lose the plot. It is the voice of a man fearful of hypocrisy. He wants to live in the world and not behind some wall. I was literally imagining the wall and the swimming pool just behind it. As I was climbing the wall to get in to voyeuristically condemn him, he was making sure he jumped over the wall and into the street where the ordinary people struggle to get by.

I was convicted. I did not live behind any particularly wealthy walls, but it might be easier for me, who was relatively speaking still a rich Westerner, to make no effort to see what was on my level without jumping walls. I was also provoked to look at my Christian walls. Was I hiding behind them? The song ended with me desiring to follow Browne headlong into a world that is full of beauty yet mixed with cruelty, seeing birth happening alongside all kinds of devastation and surrounded always with the possibility of change. I wanted to get out from inside my soul or behind my safe theological fortress. I wanted to live in the world, not inside some church, where it would be so much easier to hide away from the world. Browne had moved me deep within my spiritual walk to get engaged with the world that my God loves passionately. I prayed that God would allow me and give me the courage to become alive in the world!

I can remember speaking in Trinity College University Dublin. The talk I was giving was being held in the Students Union, and as I spoke, I gazed wall to wall at all the posters for many of the societies in the university. There were campaigns for victims of AIDS, for injustices in East Timor, for famine relief emergencies in Africa, for battered women on the streets of Dublin itself. As I spoke about how the Christians could be salt and light in their university, there seemed to be so many opportunities for those who claimed that their hearts beat with the same compassion as Jesus to get involved. Yet they had been conditioned in their home churches to think of these other societies as enemies and outsiders who had nothing to do with them. They had been taught to build walls around those who believed like they did and to block out any who had different opinions about God. To be alive in the world had been openly discouraged. Let it go down its merry way to destruction outside the walls. Instead they were to consume themselves with events and programs and people inside their walls. It reminded me of my friend Gordon's disgust when he attended Sunday worship on World AIDS Day to find no mention of the sub Sahara African pandemic. It was outside the walls; ignore it. Let us preach on more effective ways to read your Bible and pray for our missionaries in Malawi as they save souls from eternal damnation.

Looking East was the album that Jackson Browne was touring at the time of the Botanic Gardens concert, and it could be an umbrella term for his entire thirty-year career, as from his Pacific seashore, he gazes across the entire continent to seek out what are the issues and what might be the solutions to the times in which he lives and creates. It and its follow-up, 2002's *The Naked Ride Home,* are good albums to assess the prophetic vision of Jackson Browne. There is an abundance of social protest, political rage, romantic yearnings, and spiritual searching. From his place of observing the outside, Browne has always been the most acute at the personal introspection where change begins, and then in recent days he has had a new awareness of the need for the personal connection that stokes the potential within all of us to do something about that world that we see when we look out from our walls.

Looking East is a powerful vignette of a country full of hungry souls, and we are not talking about simply those without food. The hunger is greater and deeper than three square meals. This is a hunger that is as ravenous in the mansion and the banquet. This is a hunger that is all day, everywhere, and deeply rooted inside everybody. The famine is not for money or entertainment or power. No, it is the soul that is suffering this famine while our hedonistic tendencies for greed and lust are having a sensory overload. Augustine said that every human being had a hole in the soul that only God could fill. Browne describes it as "a God sized hunger" seeping through all the crisis of the generation.

Browne would later call the America he gazes across a "Casino Nation." This is concentrated stuff with Browne packing in his views on the media, commerce, fame, gambling, and the justice system under the shadow of a nation that claims to be under the Lordship of Jesus but is obsessed with producing arms. The "fabled crucible of the free world," he describes it, and ultimately the punch line is that man serves the entire infrastructure of the nation rather than the infrastructure serving man. It echoes Jesus' suggestion of how the Pharisees had hijacked the Sabbath and burdened the people beneath that which should have benefited them.

Browne had always been "Alive In The World" and active in campaigning. But although his music skirted the corners of socio-political commentary in the '70s in songs like "Before The Deluge" and "Everyman," it was the *No Nukes* concerts at the end of 1979 that changed the fulcrum of his muse towards the open lettered protesting of his '80s work. Inspired by his mother who marched against the Vietnam War, Browne seems to have always had an outspokenness lying dormant within. Now and again there would be little eruptions. In his biography, *The Story Of A Hold Out*, Rich Wiseman notes an outburst in the early '70s when during a concert in Hempstead, New York, Browne is riled by the seeming indifference to a remark about the Vietnam War soon being finished. He lashes out at the indifference, "Southeast where? That's not in New York ... Southeast Asia. It's not in New Jersey either ... For all we know Southeast Asia is some mythical place, cooked up by the *New York Times*. I don't think so, though. I happen to think it's maybe a real place where real people live, try to live."[1]

That ignorance of the actions carried out in the name of the American people is what Browne would spend the next ten years exposing. When his government began to get involved in underhand maneuvers in Central America, Browne was not going to sit back and say nothing. This is the "weapon producing nation under Jesus" using their arsenal in the most unjust way imaginable. It was a time when the ghost of Woody Guthrie was well and truly alive again with many rock artists getting particularly enraged by the CIA's support of right wing fascist regimes in Central America. Little Steven from Springsteen's E Street Band was making political rock kick. Jackson Browne even covered his song "Voice Of America" on the B-side of "In The Shape Of A Heart," the love song from the industrial political jive of "Lives In The Balance" and "I Am A Patriot" on *World In Motion*. Bruce Cockburn, a Canadian, stuck his oar in and started to highlight (on radio stations that would take the risk) just exactly what the nation was doing.

At one concert Browne prefaces "Lives In The Balance" with this mini-sermon, "This is a song about Central America and about the United States ... (long pause) sometimes I just don't know what to say ... you know ... I ah ... I want to sing you this song. It seems there should be something in addition, you know something more, something more that could be said, something more that could be done because ... I tell you it's very ... it's very confusing because what we say we're doing and what we're actually doing are two very different things. What we say we're doing in central America is we're opposing communism but if you look at the history of the last two hundred years or the last fifty years what we've done is we've supported a lot of military dictatorships and I don't know if that is the best way to oppose communism. It seems to me if you wanted to stop communism you would give those people democracy. I guess I give you this song with the fervent belief that its not too late to do the right thing in Central America. I'd like to dedicate this song to the women and children who have been killed in the war against Nicaragua to date. Of course Nicaragua is a country that we are technically at peace with but 40 percent of the death toll of this CIA war have been women and children."

Communism was the great demon of America in the latter half of the twentieth century. Anyone who was coloring slightly outside the lines was branded a communist to whip up general opposition to whatever. Even as recently as March 2003, a news presenter in America was accusing the European Press, and even the more conservative British newspaper, *The Daily Telegraph,* of being Communist simply because they were asking serious questions about George W. Bush and Tony Blair's decision to go to war with Iraq. The Berlin wall had crumbled well over a decade earlier, and still Americans in the public eye were suspicious of this mythical enemy.

There are a few dangers of such paranoia. Firstly, many people get condemned for being something that they are not. Secondly, Marxism, which was the formative ideology of Communism, is lost to Christians who would do well to engage with his analysis. A student came to my office recently and was perturbed as he wanted to write his paper on Marx without compromising his Christian stand and was finding things in Marx that he could not disagree with. Had he lost his faith? Marx became public enemy number one with his dismissal of "religion as the opiate of the people." It is interesting to note that he is dismissing religion in general and not Christianity in particular, and it may have to be asked if his critique had been deserved. Ignoring everything else he wrote because of this and a few other ideas that clash with Christian belief means we miss his strong ethical dimension and his overriding concern with justice and standing for the poor and marginalized. It was not Marx but the early Church who came up with the idea that those who had would give to those who have not, but now we dismiss the biblical truth because Marx said it![2] He had his own vision of Mitchell's Woodstock, The Old Testament's Garden of Eden, and Jesus' kingdom of heaven, though some of his methodology was in error, many of the things he said need a real examination.

That is the final danger. We miss the opportunity of sharpening our beliefs and working out our actions on the stone of his critique. Whether it is faith or the political decisions of government, Browne believes that "the role of an artist in society is to ask questions and make us think and confront us with what's going on." As a Christian, the first line in "Casino Nation," *a weapons producing nation under Jesus*, is enough for a week of ponderings. What a contradiction? Yet, is it not true? What an indictment!

Browne's biggest indictment of Jesus came in his song "The Rebel Jesus." On a Bruce Cockburn Christmas special in 1993, Browne introduces the song he wrote for the Chieftains' Christmas album *The Bells Of Dublin*. He speaks of how he had been very much looking forward to singing a traditional Christmas carol for that particular project but could not find his voice. He then says a Mayan Indian friend of his told him to write his own. He goes on, "We had also been talking about Christianity and the impact of Christianity on the Mayan people and somehow the two things got combined into this Christmas song. I didn't really mean to, but it came out as an indictment of Christianity. I just want everybody to know you can indict whatever major religion you feel like indicting in this song here. I didn't mean to just lay it all at the feet of Christianity but it's also an advocacy of the teachings of Christ so I hope you take it in the spirit of which it's intended ... " At the song's end in the next little bit of tuning up, Bruce Cockburn is the first voice you hear: "I think Christianity can take an indictment like that anytime, speaking as a Christian."

They then go on to discuss with some humor Salman
Rushdie and those religions which are not so keen on such
indictments!

The song itself is a gem and does what Browne explained it
would. It indicts the dubious practices of those who claim
to follow Christ while using Him as the rule of thumb to do
so. He uses the story of Jesus over turning the tables in
the temple saying they had turned it into a "robber's den"
deliberately using the words of the rebel Jesus to describe
how we have abused nature and asks questions about the
building up of "pride and gold" in churches.

The irony of the poor being ignored on Christmas day is the
crux of the song. Browne suggests that most of those gathered
round their warm romanticized family tables on Christmas
Day do not give much time or money to those with whom
Jesus spent His life. He then takes a line from Oscar Romero,
the South American priest who said, "If I feed the poor they
call me a saint, but if I ask why the poor are poor they call me
a communist." Browne says that he would be treated the same
as the rebel Jesus.

It is necessary for us to believe that Christianity is robust
enough to take such indictments, any indictments. We must
never get to a stage where anyone who asks questions of us,
whether from inside or outside the Church, is blacklisted,
sidelined, or vilified, like so many were when they asked
questions of America's involvement in the Iraqi War.

As the planes crashed into the twin towers on that day
that changed history, we were very speedy to stand as the
righteous who had been unjustly invaded by a handful of
fanatical political zealots who felt their sad and sick cause was
not only worth dying for, but killing thousands of innocent
people in the process. Yet, those are the moments for us to
stop and remember and search ourselves for any reason for

our own repentance. The Mayan Indian that inspired Browne and in whose persona he sings "The Rebel Jesus" would have stories of those who murderously smashed their way into His people's history on equally tragic days, but in those days it was Browne's European ancestors who were the terrorists who killed his people in cold blood in the name of "The Rebel Jesus." That "Rebel Jesus" loses nothing of His divinity or redeeming and reigning power when "his people, called by his name, humble themselves and pray, seek his face and turn from their wicked ways ..." Indeed Scriptures tell us that at moments like that, God hears from heaven and heals our land. May there always be indictments that can push and shove us to such times.

There was a debate raging on the letters page of *The London Times*. What was wrong with the world? G.K. Chesterton eventually made a short, sharp, sweet contribution—"What is wrong with the world? I am." Jackson Browne is not the kind of songwriter who lists off his accusations at the world, and does not see his part in the downfall. As well as being alive in the world, he has spent his entire career asking what it means to be alive and alive in the best possible kind of condition to make a positive contribution in the world. On *The Naked Ride Home*, he has a song of self reflection, "The Night Inside Me." With a lyrical nod back to his 1974 album *Late For The Sky* while musically a descendent of 1983's *Lawyers In Love*, the night here is not a dark and foreboding place where you wait for the day, but rather a haven of calm and peace from the madness that the day brings. As Browne has done so well for almost thirty years, it begins in the most personal of introspection, but his search within himself leads him to the questions of his age—in this case the speed and thus chaos of the modern day schedule.

The chaos, he exposes, has got us by the throat. We are obeying that which we do not want to but have to. And yet he sees this other possibility. He is striving to find his place

between the world that he obeys in an out of controlled way
and this other world, a place where, he so poetically put
it, angels play. Heaven somewhere out there, a vision of an
alternative. For Browne that was Spain, where he has lived
for a period since his last record, *Looking East*. A place where
obviously he felt he escaped from that which unravels us.

Browne had started off as the songwriting psychotherapist of
"Everyman," as his second album would be called. In the era
of the songwriter, he sat alongside the James Taylors and the
Carole Kings, but always added a depth of vision that set him
apart. Browne's questions were about who he was and what
place he had in the world that was coming out of the hippy
era that had set them free, but free for what? John Lennon had
said that the dream was over, but what did that mean—going
back to the nightmare?

Browne's two classic albums, *Late for the Sky* and its follow-up
The Pretender, were albums of tender spiritual yearning. They
were the heart and soul of a young man trying to untangle
the confusion of the direction and meaning of his life. There
is lots of running down roads and highways trying to get to
somewhere, but the destination remains an elusive question
and never provides the answer. There's a little frustration
on "Farther On" where no matter how alert he is to what is
going on and how he can change it heaven doesn't seem to be
getting any closer.

The eternal seems to be what remains out of reach. As he
stands over his friends grave on "The Dancer," we are as close
to destination as that ball that hits the very top of the fencing
with all the bases loaded at the bottom of the ninth in game
seven of the World Series and drops on the wrong side. He
cannot get the song but he cannot help but listen. When these
are the questions that the peak of our pop culture is pouring
out, it can only be even more frustrating that the Church
seemed to be failing to engage with such soul searching.

If Browne fears for the eternal destination of the soul, he
was equally concerned with the soul being sucked from the
idealism of youth to leave the late twentysomethings going
through life's physical motions. For the youth of Browne's
peers, there was heightened idealism, and his best known
song "The Pretender" dealt most clearly with the hippy
implosion. It took up the theme of the previous year's "Before
The Deluge," in which he sang of the exchange of love and
the eternal for fashion and the moment. In "The Pretender,"
he was still asking what went wrong. What happened to
the dream? Where are the changes? Were they just "fitful
dreams?" Is there a greater awakening in the distance? Here
is a man who hoped for better with a claustrophobic sense
of trudge and the inevitable. He had such strong ideals in
the passion of his sixties youth but here he is surrendering.
The climax of the song is a plea for whoever is listening
on this earth or beyond this earth to say a prayer for "The
Pretender."

The Pretender though cannot make it alone. On both *Looking
East* and *The Naked Ride Home*, the maturing songwriter sees
the need for others to give him the spiritual courage to be
alive in the world and in his own soul. "Some Bridges" could
be a companion piece to "Alive In The World" as it again
deals with walking around in a "torn up world" where he
finds all kinds of desperation and poverty. The credit for his
survival is the smile of his lover, whose smile he can carry as
a symbol of the strength she gives him. That last line about
carrying her smile becomes the repeated refrain of the song.
Browne is in need of a soul mate, companionship, fellowship
in order to maintain his compassion for the poor and the
injustices of the world.

A similar theme is found on *The Naked Ride Home*'s "Never
Stop," which is again directed to a lover who has helped
him when he is weary and his "train was off the track." It
is a song of encouragement and yet there is a need in his

encouragement to be a spiritual resource in the midst of that chaotic world described in "The Night Inside Me." He is near praying that she, "never stop coming up with all of that love for me" and then it goes wider than his own needs to that of us all and that we should never stop seeking the world that love is looking to bring about. Again the song ends with this smile that he has been carrying and that makes him, "the richest man I know."

The world that love wants to see. That is a thought. What might that world be? What kind of world would love conjure if it was free of the hatred that gets in the way? On an album that already seems to inhabit that space between where we obey this world's pressures and a place where the angels dance, Jackson takes us to that angelic dance floor in this song about heaven, "Don't You Want To Be There." It is a place where "the light is breaking" and where there is "a golden glow." Very much central to it in this song in particular is forgiveness. It is a place "where forgiveness rules" and a place where the listener is encouraged to go and make it right with the people he or she has wronged and to let go of the bitterness that grows when someone wronged them. If you have never thought of heaven, or if you have decided that it is not the place for you, Browne is very persuasive in his altar call; he is disbelieving that anyone would not want to go to a world of "grace and simple truth" for the hungry, the lost, and those driven mad by the injustice that has befallen them. It is the world that he believes we would all want to be alive in.

EIGHT

LET THE TRUTH STING

P hotographer Ben Curtis probably never intended to create an image that perfectly describes David Gray's spirituality. David Gray might not agree that it does, but if I was trying to capture this chapter in a pictorial way, I really could not do it better. David is sitting on an old wooden bench in the corner of an old building. The walls are aging brick, no plaster. His trendy sneakers clash with the scene. In the top left corner of the shot, there is a stained glass window. Gray, sitting with his hand to his mouth, has his eyes intensely focused straight ahead underneath the light coming through. It is the look of a thoughtful man. On the window there is a red cross and in the shape of an arch above it are the words, "JESUS LOVES YOU." It seems to have absolutely no relationship to David Gray. He does not seem at all aware of its existence or profundity. Yet it is there, whether it is his intention or not. It is a major part of the picture.[1]

More on that a little later, but first let me take you back to November 2002 as I parked the car, reached for my wife's hand, and walked toward Belfast's huge (for Northern Ireland) new Odyssey Arena. There was a strange knot of apprehension in the pit of my stomach as we walked. If I had been going to a David Gray gig five years previous, I would have been like a little child waiting for Santa Claus. Tonight there was no adrenaline running at all. The reason was that I have been a Gray fan since *Flesh*, his second album released in 1994. I can remember my mate David Dark bringing me his next release *Sell, Sell, Sell* from the States before it was available in Britain and waiting patiently for *White Ladder* when it was only available in Belfast through my very favorite and most trusted record shop Hector's House. I played "Birds Without Wings," "Let The Truth Sting," and "What Are You" on my radio show long before anyone decided to playlist "Babylon" and set in motion the most fantastic turn around in any singer's career. I was delighted of course with his phenomenal success, but here I was in a crowd of thousands of radio listeners who if you'd asked what his first album was, they would have answered *White Ladder*!

There was the size too. How could the intimacy of what Gray does connect in a venue that he described as "a big silver tin"? I had been there when his graduation to the Olympia Theatre in Dublin had surprised and almost overwhelmed him, and here he was in a venue five times bigger! Surely the music would be diluted in the vastness. From the moment Gray walked out onto the stage alone, sat down at the piano, and started an arena gig with a quiet ballad, "The Other Side," my fears disappeared instantly, and I was lost in an astonishing performance of defiance to everything that was against this concert being possible. Just as he didn't succumb to the pressures to make an album that would follow the huge sales of *White Ladder,* so he has kept that artistic integrity intact and has translated it into a spectacle more amazing for its understatement. As I returned to my car, I was trying to express to Janice that kind of feeling a child gets when they have just been to see Santa Claus. David Gray had not given us some glitzy spectacle, but three things much more impressive—great musicianship, great songs, and that David Gray voice! Success has made no difference to David Gray, apart from bigger crowds and a better bank balance. He must look at his bank statements and rub his eyes. In the summer of 2000, I was standing gazing out to sea outside the Promenade Ice Cream Shop in my favorite place on earth, Ballycastle, County Antrim, vaguely listening in the background to a cover band entertaining in the open air. A bit of Van Morrison's "Brown Eyed Girl" and Thin Lizzy's version of "Whiskey In The Jar" and then ... what's that ... that's David Gray's "Babylon." That and an appearance on *Top Of The Pops* in the midst of Britain's pathetic obsession with pretty faced fashion pop (including Kylie Minogue sounding just like she did in 1987 but her face looking as if she is now well old enough to know better) was the final recognition that Gray was no longer the property of me and my mates, after working his butt off for ten years to become an overnight phenomenon.

It is quite a story. In 1991 the young Gray released an album that was as big a threat to the throne of Bob Dylan as there has ever been. Yes, there have been many new Dylans declared over the last three decades, but *Century's End* had a spiritual, socially observant, political, and emotional punch that came with a lyrical nimbleness that really should have been declared as genius. "Let The Truth Sting" was a quite exceptional piece of poetry, and "Birds Without Wings" was the paradigm definition of indifference and moral inertia.

The follow-up record, *Flesh*, was as articulate and powerful, but the record company Hut hadn't had the cash registers ringing to match the artistic value. So for his third album, Gray moved to EMI America and released songs that seemed to be aiming at a little bit more pop accessibility. *Sell, Sell, Sell* failed to achieve anything, apart from a few covers on Irish singer Mary Black's *Shine* album. He would need the royalties, because Gray was suddenly, but not surprisingly, in a world where good loses out to sales without a record label.

Things looked bleak. And then the match turned. Like the opposition hitting the post or missing two penalties, this losing of a recording contract turned Gray's star around. He went into his bedroom and started experimenting with loops and beats and on the tightest of budgets, released a nine-track album in Ireland, where, unlike the rest of the world, he had a rabid little fan base. I am sure that though the songs were of the highest quality, he saw it as a stop gap in order to work out what might come next. It certainly succeeded in doing that. Indeed, "succeed" would become a new word in the Gray household.

Irish DJ Donal Doneen took the album to his heart, and suddenly week after week, these slow burning songs like "This Year's Love," "Babylon," and "Please Forgive Me" started picking up airplay, and because of at least a couple of discerning DJs in the world today and a whole lot of word of mouth, *White Ladder* became a slow burning seller that turned into an eight times platinum raging fire. That first gig in the prestigious Olympia Theatre in Dublin during this phase of growing popularity suffered a little from being his first big venue concert, but I was amazed to see a sell-out audience sing every word with an enthusiasm that would not have been out of place at a Britney concert. By this stage, Gray too must have been somewhat disbelieving. From his career grinding to a halt and the emotional struggle of his parents splitting up, he was now on the cusp of the big time. Soon his album would be cracking other territories, and the rest is history, culminating in *Top Of The Pops* and County Antrim cover bands—6.5 million sales to be precise!

When he released *A New Day At Midnight* in 2002, it raced

ahead of greatest hits compilations by Nirvana and Manic
Street Preachers, as well as U.K. pop idol Gareth Gates to
number one in the U.K. charts. The inspiration for the song
cycle was the death of Gray's father from cancer. That his wife
was pregnant during the recording process must also have
played its part, but his daughter Ivy's birth just two months
before the album's release will probably not kick in until the
follow-up album. As a result, this album is darker than *White
Ladder*, very introspective and personal, and yet dealing with
all the issues that have been making Gray's work deeper and
higher and wider than his peers for almost ten years.

We are left here with the musings of the big questions set
in the heart of sadness and loss. In the raw soul ends of
mourning, Gray becomes acutely more aware of the futility
of how and why we are living our lives. On "Freedom" he
sings about a world that is lost and who like mice on a tread
mill are captive to "the running boards." On "Real Love," the
world is a glorious fake and he is a man struggling to deal with
reality. That same song takes a Joni Mitchell hope and dream
and hears a cry of Eden much the same as the Canadian's
Woodstock recognized that we needed to get back to the way
it was in the beginning.

We are back to that photograph. Gray claims in interviews
that he has no belief in God or the afterlife, but he is not
afraid to recognize the need within us all to wish for it, even
if we do not believe in it or believe that it is not there. As well
as the wishes of Eden in "Real Love," he is seeking to meet
his loved ones somewhere beyond on "The Other Side" and
so adds his name to a list of songwriters singing about a hope
for beyond the grave. Within weeks either side of *A New Day
At Midnight*'s release, various artists would coincidently also
release songs with a similar theme; the title track of Steve
Earle's politically volatile *Jerusalem* record was a vision of
the day when the lion and the lamb lie down together; Tracy
Chapman gets very close to writing a companion piece to

Gray's "The Other Side" with "Say Hallelujah" on her *Let It Rain* album; Jackson Browne is asking "Don't You Want To Be There" in a heavenly place where all this world's ills are healed; and Bruce Springsteen touches consistently on the idea of resurrection in the aptly titled "The Rising." Elsewhere on "Last Boat To America," Gray the agnostic is wondering if there might not be something to explain the mysteries: an "unseen hand."

When I first got to hear David Gray around 1994, I did not think agnostic; I was convinced that he was a Presbyterian like me! *Century's End* was so saturated with songs of the spirit and of truth that I believed that something of a faith thing was going down. Then I heard "Birds Without Wings," and it was case proven. Here was a song about fancy wrappings on empty packages and about a people who had lost any imagination for the way forward because they spend all their time looking back. It seemed to me that this could be a zealous young believer pouring out his angst to those church elders who were doing things the way they had always been done.

To a stark acoustic strum creating an empty energyless mood, Gray asks a people out of step with the times to hoist a new flag. Maybe the images of trumpets and judgment give it a more biblical feel than he intended, but as he looks and sees *tired ideas and birds without wings,* you are left thinking that he might find some new fellowship with drums and Power Point images that seem to satisfy, if sometimes only for a short time the enthusiasm and naiveté of youth.

That it is not about the Church does not free us from its judgment. Indeed if anything, it is those who have belief in dreaming dreams and seeing visions that should be casting off the tired ideas and being an energizing force within our society for the change that Gray suggests we need, as the cat gets ready to pounce on those "birds without wings." In "lack luster times," can followers of Jesus dare to say that they have had hard days at work that make them too tired to do anything about how the world is and to care for those who are suffering as a result? To care is the Church's reason to exist. In biblical times, the Church was the social welfare system and if the government of the new laissez-faire West should be conned into thinking that "to share is to lose," followers of Christ should be those who know that it is only in the sharing, in the restoring of the fractured landscape, that there is any hope of winning.

By 2003, Gray would look back at these early songs and say, "Some of those early songs feel too naive. I can't wear them with confidence anymore."[2] In the political uncertainty and friction of the Iraqi war though, he has been dusting off "Birds Without Wings." He started dropping it into the set again in the European leg of his world tour when he needed some more "ranty ones." Interestingly, in an interview published the same week as Gray was confessing discomfort in his youthful naiveté Bono was sharing how he had been to an Anton Corbijn exhibition and seen a photograph of himself as a twenty-one-year-old. He said, "There was a look in the eye that was very striking. I think it was naivety."[3] Bono goes on to say that a journalist then asked him what he would say to that young man starting out, and Bono's reply is quite amazing. He says, "You're right. And there is no arrogance in that remark because I was right in a way then more than I am now. Because you learn fear. You learn to watch your step. You sacrifice your innocence for experience. You think that that is what will make you a better writer. You think that, but you're wrong. Clarity is what makes you a better writer; clear thinking. You have all that in your first face."[4]

A song in Gray's first face that he might now think a little naïve but that has been a constant challenge and near mission statement to me for some ten years now is "Let The Truth Sting." Those lines *Into lies ruin disease/ Into wounds*

like these/ Let the truth sting immediately had my biblically
conditioned mind thinking of Jesus telling His followers that
they were the salt of the earth.[5] Salt has healing qualities
not so much used in the modern day of more accurate and
powerful medicines. Even though the truth as salt is a more
powerful image, I need to ask myself if I am embellishing
Gray's work to fit my own language and thoughts. Maybe
he just meant medicine. The memory of my mother putting
antiseptic into a deep soccer inflicted cut on the knee when I
was eight years of age still brings water to the eye; it stung!

Whatever Gray meant and whatever standpoint he was
coming from, the truth of the truth stinging is no less true,
no less of a challenge. In many ways I find it an even bigger
challenge for those of us who at some point in our lives
decided that as we wake up every morning we would
endeavor to follow Jesus of Nazareth. He did say, "You are the
salt of the earth." He did say, "You are the light of the world."[6]
We do need to let the truth that we claim to believe in seep
into the world around us to counteract the lies, the ruin, and
the disease and bring a healing that will be to the benefit of
the whole of society.

It is always prudent to ask what wounds the salt is stinging
and where the light is shining. If nature calls loud and clear
and you wake up in a strange house in the middle of a dark
night at the height of winter, you are very dependent on the
bedside light to negotiate the way to where the call of nature
can be answered. If you reach out and flick the switch and no
light comes on, who do you scream your anger toward? Do
you give off to the night for being dark, or to the electricity
or bulb for not shining? The truth is that we expect little from
the dark but darkness. Light on the other hand is expected to
shine. Those of us whom Jesus looked at and nicknamed "the
light of the world" need to be constantly assessing if we are
little lights making one big light away from the darkness, or if
we are anywhere near to the lies, ruin, and disease that need

to feel the truth sting.

Certainly David Gray's work ever since this first scream across the bows of the world has been a search for truth, to find it and rub it into the reality of his social and political observations that would clearly reveal lies, ruin, and disease. Indeed, it was quite a statement for a songwriter to be singing in the early years of the '90s. This was eight years away from the 2000 and millennium syndrome. This was a debut album by an early twenties rookie. U2 had been trying to lighten up, and people had had enough of singers trying to make a difference. In some ways looking back, Gray was just born for the wrong time. Hut was brave to give him a chance. Long gone were the days when talent overcame fashion. If Gray had been a peer of Jackson Browne, there would not have been a wait of some eight years before he hit the spot.

What is it that Gray defines as the wounds of society, and what is the truth that will sting such "lies, ruin, disease"? Gray's first three albums are crammed full of his naming of the powers of our late twentieth century malaise. He lists them off like machine gun fire, too many to take in one session of continued listening. On "Let The Truth Sting" itself, we have tradition, repetition, rigmarole, plastic innocence, emptiness, appearances, hollow applause, numbness, godlessness, delusion's regime, violence, TV, money, stubborn clenched fists, hatred, and crumbling beauty.

There are recurring themes through those first three albums that when listened to in any intensive kind of way would pound your soul with challenge, rebuke, inspiration, and hopeful resistance more than a lifetime of sermons. The soul searching is almost overwhelming. Narcissism is certainly one of Gray's most sung about lies. The shallowness of the beauty of skin and the danger of succumbing to the power of the mirror's persuasion is everywhere. In "Let The Truth Sting" itself, Gray elaborates on the pain in his stomach as he looks at people's vain attempts to prevent the encroachment of age and thus the erosion of their beauty. In "Century's End," there are "faces made of wax" but more sinister is a society obsessed with the outward appearance while the soul is decaying." On "Folk Song" off *Sell, Sell, Sell* he is again ranting against the folly of beauty.

Though this obviously has to do with the late twentieth and early twenty-first century obsession with physical beauty as defined by culture through fashion magazines and the perfectly defined shapes and complexions of pop and Hollywood, there is a bigger picture of a society that looks good on the surface, but lurking underneath are the ruin and disease. From politicians to big businesses to social structures, everyone is trying to cover over the cracks of a society that is sick deep within its soul.

Gray is not satisfied in just exposing the lies, ruin, and disease. He needs to find healing. He is defiantly shouting to "let the truth sting." There is a great deal of defiance in his work and always the almost naïve suggestion that we should have faith and hope in the possibility of a "New Horizon." He dismisses those who have no interest in such a mission. In "Forever Is Tomorrow Is Today," he is pushing aside the doubters and the apathetic, telling them to get out of the way if they cannot see any hope in an echo of Dylan's "The Times They Are A-Changing." In "Birds Without Wings," he has no time for those who come with their excuses; being too tired to bother has no place in a world where there is more to it than sustaining the fancy wrappings of wealth and security. He is incredulous towards such inhumane soulless responsibility. There are many such things that threaten to suck the blood form the veins of living and revolutionary hope and defiance.

"New Horizon" is the song where Gray lays out the foundation of hope. The enemy to the reality of the "New Horizon" beginning is complacency which can be vicious and imprison our compassion. Complacency is not some passive sin of omission without effects. It is a vicious killer of the hope of tomorrow. On "Sell, Sell, Sell" he is looking to a religious image of a candle of defiance ... and to those who do not want to make a difference he begs to differ.

Where the future lies with Gray seems to be in imagination. We have already spent time with those "Birds Without Wings" who lack imagination, and on "Forever Is Tomorrow Is Today" he is pontificating that we "need a vision" and to "shatter the eyes of stone" On *Flesh*'s "What Are You," he accuses the maintainers of the old ways to have given up imagination for a few "pounds and pence." This it would seem is where the ruin of society rests. Jesus never said that money was evil, but He did warn us that it was the root of all evil or at least the majority of it. It distracts us from our true purpose, it sucks our souls dry of living, it deludes us into thinking we have a route to happiness in material things. It is the cause of crime ("Century's End") and always leaves us with a dissatisfied taste of the ultimately unattainable ("Faster Sooner Now").

Without a doubt, this materialism and financial security and decadence at the feet of profit margin cannot, in Gray's vision of the future, bring any kind of salvation. It does not have the transcendent power that Gray knows we need. That brings us right back to the question of Gray's belief or agnosticism. Does he want to believe or does he need to believe? Is there a mysterious mystical entity behind the universe that he is just too frightened to name or define? He does say, *you are trying to spell what the wind can't explain* ("Coming Down"), and that elusive power does permeate his work, lies below his skin, and ignites all his energy to let the truth sting in the world where he resides. As he puts it on "Silver Lining" from *White Ladder,* we were born innocent and this world's madness has dragged us down so we need to reassess and redirect our focus to reinvest our lives in the only things worth living for—"innocence and magic, amen!"

NINE

LAND OF HOPE AND DREAMS

I t had been fifteen years since I had been to a Bruce
Springsteen concert. The last time was in 1985 on a warm
day by the river Boyne when he rocked Slane Castle on
the opening concert of the European leg of his world
domination tour. With *Born In The USA*'s steady string of
radio friendly singles, 65,000 ticket sales had never been
easier, and Dave Marsh suggests that another 35,000 were so
taken by Bruce's denting of the charts that they got in without
a ticket.[1] That 85,000 of the crowd looked confused when he
played "Rosalita" left us self-righteous and true fans a little
angry, but truth be told I was only introduced by my mate
Rab after *Darkness On The Edge Of Town*. It was an amazing
spectacle, and for sure the man who had been so famously
dubbed "the future of rock 'n' roll" and who got his face on
the cover of *Time* and *Newsweek* ten years earlier was now
very much the present. Playing for so long that support acts

could not find time in the schedule, Springsteen made us all feel "Born To Run," each and every one of us pulling out of the "Badlands" to win in a "Promised Land" somewhere down the highway.

Now in 1999, here I was again, older and less obsessive, a point proven when I did not buy a ticket to see him on the *Ghost Of Tom Joad* tour when he played half a mile away from my home. But the E Street Band was back, and like a burning bush in the wilderness, it intrigued me. Needless to say, there were no disappointments, but as we got to marvel at one of the most gifted bunch of rock musicians ever assembled, it was a chance to ponder: How and where was the Boss at fifty? The running along the extended stage had slowed to a canter. The show was down from three hours and forty-five minutes to a still generous two hours and forty-five minutes. Yet the playing benefited from the maturity, and the songs were in many cases reinvented with the wisdom of the years, especially "Born In The USA." The greatly misunderstood fist-punching, sky stomper of Slane Castle was now a slide guitar folk song whose message was a little more explicit.

Then there was the epiphany, the surprise, the twist in the tale. "Land Of Hope and Dreams," the brand new encore, became more like a closing hymn and left me reassessing this gig and Springsteen's career in the most spiritual of ways. The song has two much older brothers. Curtis Mayfield's "People Get Ready" has been the subject of cover versions from Bob Dylan to U2 to Jeff Beck and Rod Stewart, and Springsteen was readily acknowledging the relationship by dropping bits of it into "Land Of Hope and Dreams" on his 2003 tour. Woody Guthrie starts and ends his book *Bound For Glory* with the template that Springsteen uses. Interestingly though, Guthrie's train *don't carry no gamblers/ Liars thieves and big-shot ramblers*. Bruce gets his Christian grace theology a whole lot better as his train picks up passengers on its road to glory, heaven, another land where saints, sinners, losers, winners,

whores, gamblers, and as Dylan put it in another sibling of
the song, "every hung out person" would one day hear the
"Chimes of Freedom." Springsteen of course sang that Dylan
song as the theme tune of the 1988 Amnesty Tour.

Maybe I should have seen it coming. Springsteen has always
had his spiritual imagery. Redemption, the Promised Land,
saints and sinners have always been part of his songwriting
landscape, but it seems that as his career goes on, the more
it becomes the driving force, rather than just a treasury of
good ideas and rhymes. Grace is a big word in his vocabulary
when explaining the songs. Tonight there was almost a
feeling of church, both in the strength of fellowship on the
stage and in the bonding of the crowd in some communal
belief in something joyous. "If I Should Fall Behind" seems
to have become central to this particular reunion tour. From
a very powerful love song, it has grown into a community
commitment piece, with his E Street band comrades Lofgren,
Van Zant, Patti, and Clarence taking verses along with Bruce.
What could have been a little bit corny and sentimental
turned into an epic statement of friendship, a subject again
that has littered Springsteen's work since he first sent
greetings from Asbury Park.

Springsteen had been taking on the persona of a preacher
throughout the show, but until "Land Of Hope And Dreams,"
I had been swaying between him being sacrilegious or
serious. The DVD of the tour *Live In New York City* gave an
opportunity to put the content of the sermons under much
closer scrutiny. As the band gets up as mighty a head of
steam as any other rock band ever could, we enter the home
stretch, from "Badlands" into "Tenth Avenue Freeze Out" and
on into "Born To Run," three songs from the '70s when the
legend was coined. "Badlands" is the place where we need
to escape, and "Born To Run" is what Springsteen has called
"summational and continues to be summational of all the
ideas I have had. It's always had a spiritual element, I think

the end of it where we get to the place where we wanna go ...
that is what all our music is about ..."[2]

"Tenth Avenue Freeze Out" in the middle here gives us
clues to where we want to go, not in the song itself, but in a
trademark Springsteen improvised spoken word rant. In the
old days, these would have been stories of him, his father,
and their constant quarreling, but in the latter days, they are
invariably these little revivalist sermonettes. This is no ad
lib. This is a man who is putting the very core of his art into a
humorous but deadly serious monologue ...

I want to go to that riverside
I want to find that river of life
I want to find that river of love
I want to find that river of faith
And that river of hope
Tonight I want to go to that river of transformation
Where you can go and be changed
But you've got to work at it, that's right
I want to go to that river of sanctification
Where all of life's graces and blessings
Can fall down upon you like rain
But you've got to work at it
I want to go to that river of resurrection
Where everyone gets a second chance
But you've got to work at it
Tonight I want to go to that river of sexual healing and
companionship
I want to find that river of joy
And that river of happiness
I'm not bullsh—ing back here
But you don't just stumble on to those things
You don't find those places by accident
You've got to seek them out and search after them
And that's why we're here night after night after night after
night

Because you can't get to those things by yourself
You got to have help
But that's where I want to go tonight
And I want you to go with me
Because I need to go with you
That's why I'm here
And tonight I want to throw a rock n roll exorcism
A rock n roll baptism
And a rock n roll bar mitzvah
That's right, we're gonna do it all tonight
Everything, right here
I want them waters to fall down on me
And set me free, set you free

There is a wonderful moment when Springsteen, having
been walking across the front of the altar addressing his
congregation, turns back toward the E Street Church Choir.
He says those words, "I'm not bullsh–ting back here," and at
that moment the camera catches his wife Patti and longest
dearest friend, Little Steve Van Zandt. Van Zandt seems to be
whispering "Amen brother," but there is something in his eye
that gives off the vibe of this all being a mischievous joke.
Bruce, though, is not kidding. It took him almost thirty years,
but Bruce Springsteen has finally found a place to take all
those alienated tramps, racing drivers, and their lovers.

Springsteen's train of "Land of Hope and Dreams" is actually
full of every character and song that Springsteen has ever
written about, a veritable collection of saints and the sinners.
He and Tom Waits have been the two songwriters to most
poetize the kind of marginalized people who Jesus sought out
and had the most time for. They have, on the whole, given
these characters the very sympathy and hope that Jesus did.
Jesus never judged them or damned them to hell the way
He did the religious and self-righteous. And here they all are
filling the carriages and heading toward the light, leaving all
that darkness in albums gone by, heading for the place where

the character in "The Ghost Of Tom Joad" was waiting for a time "when the first would be last and the last would be first."

Born To Run was the moment Bruce Springsteen came of age artistically. His first two albums had not exactly set the charts of the world alight, but on *Born To Run*, he brought everything that had influenced him into one intoxicating mix that was simply a landmark album in the history of rock 'n' roll. Springsteen was now, as Jon Landau said, "the future of rock 'n' roll." Yet, at the same time in his own personal life, Springsteen came of age much further along.

There seems to have been a turning point in Springsteen's personal development at the time of most upheaval. In the mid-'80s, he released *Nebraska*, putting out stark naked four-track demos that captured his storytelling in the most satisfying of ways. He then proceeded to make the monster *Born In The USA* and conquered the world commercially. In double quick time, he had married model Julianne Phillips and just as fast wrote the "all is far from well in love" album *Tunnel Of Love*, got himself divorced, and hooked up with Patti Scialfa, his new backing singer!

It was in these years that Springsteen's paradigm shifted, and he literally did come of age. In the untangling of life's major issues—marriage, divorce, and becoming the most famous rock star on the planet—he seemed to make sense of all the questions that *Born To Run* had raised. Introducing the reworked acoustic version of the song during the *Tunnel Of Love* tour he said, "This is a song I guess that has changed a lot over the years as I've sung it ... I guess when I wrote this song I thought I was writing about a guy and a girl that wanted to run and keep on running and never come back. And that was a, that was a nice romantic idea but I realized that after I put all those people in all those cars I was going to have to figure out some place for them to go. And I realized that in the end I guess that individual freedom when it's not connected to some sort of community or friends or the world outside ends up feeling pretty meaningless. So, I guess that guy and that girl they were out there looking for connection and I guess that's what I'm doing here tonight. So, this is a song about two people trying to find their way home. I'd like to do it for you and dedicate it to you. Just saying this song has kept me good company on my search and I hope it's kept you good company on yours."

As he spoke these words, he was standing on the border about to cross over and head on into the '90s part of his journey that would take him toward that land of hopes and dreams. Three major themes have been running concurrently throughout Springsteen's career; the dream of escape and the search for the place where escape should be heading; the move from his own individual isolation to a sense of connection as a husband, father, and friend; and the transformation in his religious imagery from an Old Testament judgmental God to a New Testament understanding of grace, rebirth, and that relational possibility with the transcendent as with fellow human beings. It is a fascinating journey where the myth of song, the reality of life, and his philosophy of life and faith run alongside each other intrinsically connected.

Springsteen was always an outsider. He would tell James Henke in a 1992 interview in *Rolling Stone*, "I am an isolationist by nature."[3] He admits to Henke that he was unhappy due to his relationships particularly with women—"They always ended poorly; I didn't know how to have a relationship with a woman." He later would say how the failure of his first marriage was his fault—"I didn't know how to be a husband."[4]

Christopher Sandford makes this a powerful subplot of his biography *Point Blank*. It is not that Sandford is attempting any kind of Albert Goldman character assassination; it is simply that he is telling the story. You do not need to know

much about Springsteen to know that he did not get along
with his father. The box set *Live/1975-85* has a few yarns that
highlight the sense of being an outcast in his own home. The
young Bruce believed that the two things most hated in his
home were him and his guitar and that his dad cut his hair
when he was laid up after a bike crash.

It seems that school was no sense of relief or place to find
identity and compensate for the lack of connection in his
house. The nuns are said to have shoved him in a garbage bin
and also tried to encourage his classmates to refuse to let him
graduate because of the length of his hair and general state.
His shy disposition did not allow him to find, as many others
did, a place of notoriety among his peers.

Sandford does not see this social incompetence as ending
when Springsteen did find his identity as the "future of
rock 'n' roll." Springsteen's prolific songwriting, four-hour
stage shows, and general workaholic lifestyle were to keep
the world out and the reality of his relational deficiencies
at bay. If Sandford stretches one point a little bit thin and a
whole lot too tabloid demeaning in his book, it is the serial
womanizing of Springsteen's early '80s. It seems his mother,
like all mothers, was concerned about her son settling down.
Maybe it is not just to prove Sandford right, but only when
he resolved the issue of his life partner and eventually got
together with Scailfa, who he casually dated before marrying
Phillips, that Springsteen settled into maturity. There seems to
have been a certain loneliness about Springsteen, a coldness
of soul even while he was partying and guesting on Asbury
Park stages and writing songs for whoever wanted them.

Alongside this was the lack of redemption in Springsteen's
work. Yes, he was "born to run," "pulling out of here to win"
("Thunder Road") and believed in the "Promised Land." And
yes, he told us on "Badlands" that he did believe in love and
faith and that he did pray that salvation might release him

from the Badlands. Yet, still there was a sense of doom and damnation that seems rooted in Old Testament and inevitable judgment. As Bill Flanagan wrote in his introduction to the Springsteen interview in his *Written On My Soul* book in 1986, "Springsteen does not expect redemption to come from above. He accepts the fall into sin more easily than the promise of heaven. When God comes out from between the lines of Springsteen songs to make an appearance, it's inevitably the vengeful God of the Old Testament, an Almighty who could do man no greater favor than to leave him alone."[5]

The characters in *Nebraska* have as bleak an outlook as the cover photograph of a barren landscape through the windscreen of a car. In his introduction to the lyrics of the album in his book, *Songs*, Springsteen speaks about his influences coming from the "painful plainness" of his early family memories and the writing of Flannery O'Connor, whose stories "reminded him of the unknowability of God and contained a dark spirituality that resonated with my own feelings at the time."[6] He "wanted the blood on it to feel destined and fateful."[7] He succeeded in a list of characters and stories that maybe have the perfect conclusion to their fate in the title track, based on the Terence Malick movie *Badlands*, which tells the story of Charles Starkweather and Caril Fugate driving from Nebraska to Wyoming, killing ten people as they went. Journalist Mikal Gilmore, whose brother was also the serial killer Gary Gilmore, suggested that Springsteen "neither seeks their redemption nor asks for their judgment." Surely judgment is clear in "Starkweather," as the killer realizes he is without doubt guilty, but that also, there is something outside him that damns the entire human race—"a meanness in this world."

Maybe a look over the shoulder to "Adam Raised a Cain" on *Darkness On The Edge Of Town* would clear up the theology of this phase in the Jersey Devil's career. Cain slays his brother and is cast into the east of Eden and Springsteen then somehow links that event to all of us now paying for somebody else's transgression. This is a poetic and succinct doctrine of mankind's fall from the place of grace that Adam and Eve knew in the Garden of Eden as narrated in the first three chapters of Genesis. Though banished from the Garden before the first murder in human history, it would be the fate of us all to live outside that blessed Garden with all the benefits of a close relationship with our creator, a vocation as His co-workers, and the inheritance of His most perfect creation.

St. Paul's letter to the Christians in Rome would give a longer treatise on the destiny of man and woman as a result of the goings on in Eden. The apostle's theory is that it is the result of Adam's sin that we all sin, and in the condemnation of Adam we are all condemned. Paul does give the other side of the Christian hope—that we can all be forgiven through the death of the one man Jesus, making Jesus some kind of second Adam.[8] Springsteen leaves the hope out of the mix at this point of his spiritual development, but there is that flicker of light as he signs off from signs off from *Nebraska* with "Reason to Believe."

Between *Nebraska* and the release of *Human Touch* and *Lucky Town* on the very same day in 1992, Springsteen finds more of that reason to believe. During the *Tunnel Of Love* Tour, he literally found the avenue of his salvation—backing singer Patti Scailfa. Everything Bruce Springsteen has done has been different since he fell in love and consequently married and started a family with his "red headed woman." Springsteen's notes on *Human Touch* and *Lucky Town* in his lyric book *Songs* tell us that he didn't do much musically for two years. He explains the theme, "On the songs "Soul Driver" and "Real World" on *Human Touch*, people search to find some emotional contact, some modest communion, some physical and sexual connection. But to receive what love delivers, they have to surrender themselves to each other and accept fate.

This tension is at the heart of *Human Touch*."[9]

These albums are drenched in a new language and mind-set in the Springsteen canon. His tone in relation to God is an antithesis of before. "I Wish I Were Blind" and "Living Proof" are filled with grace and God reflection. In the latter, on an ordinary night as his child cries in his mother's arms, he finds "the Lord's undying light," and in trying to describe the sacred moment, finds "a little bit of God's mercy" which is his living proof. Make the most of such times he suggests as he encourages his wife that they should suck the marrow from "the treasures of the Lord."

Forgiveness has become a replacement for the inevitability of damnation. Though on "The Long Goodbye," there seems to be little evidence of its arrival as the singer is still waiting to find God's forgiveness whereas on "Book Of Dreams" he is "drinking in" the very same forgiveness. There is a sacred light shining in "My Beautiful Reward" and prayers going up in his song about the first Gulf war, "Souls Of The Departed."

In that previously quoted and very revealing interview with James Henke, he speaks very clearly about how Patti had the patience and the wisdom to deal with his troubles. Children too had been a profound conversion event for Springsteen, as indeed it is for most human beings. Henke asks him about the toughest thing about being a father, and he responds, "Engagement, engagement, engagement."[10] We are suddenly thrown into that place of connection that he spoke about when introducing "Born To Run." Then he goes on, "You're afraid to love something so much, you're afraid to be that in love. Because a world of fear leaps upon you, particularly in the world that we live in. But then you realize: 'Oh I see, to love something so much, as much as I love Patti and my kids, you've got to be able to accept and live with that world of fear, that world of doubt, of the future. And you've got to give it all today and not hold back.' And that was specialty; my specialty was keeping my distance so that if I lost something, it wouldn't hurt that much. And you can do that, but you're never going to have anything."[11]

The real life drama of Springsteen's life that we have become involved in here is very similar to a parable Jesus told called The Prodigal Son, the title of an unreleased Springsteen song. In Luke 17 Jesus tells a story about a son who in many ways sees himself as being "born to run." He wants to get out of his "town for losers," and he takes his inheritance and "bursts out of here to win." After a life of depraved hedonistic hell raising, he ends up penniless and eating the food he is feeding the pigs on a farm. A moment of epiphany hits him that life back home might be a whole lot better than this, and he heads for home. His relationship with his father needs to change, he needs a place to belong, and he is at the mercy of his father's forgiveness or judgment. It is Jesus' most remarkable story of grace, as the Prodigal, no doubt filled with fear and apprehension, steps onto the lane leading to his dad's farmhouse. What must have been running through his mind? How will he explain? What reception will he get? How bad will the judgment be? As he takes those apprehensive steps, his father sees him. He has been watching and longing for his return the entire time. Seeing his son, he races down the lane in the most undignified fashion and throws his arms around the wretched waster, puts a ring on his finger, and throws a party. It is a remarkable and wonderful response to wayward living. It is a glimpse into the heart of God.

I have no idea where Bruce is in that story, but after the run, he had his epiphany, and he headed for a destination, looking for a home. His life was transformed. His relationship with his father was transformed. He found grace and love and belonging. He even longed for spiritual fellowship when again to John Henke he admitted, "Like I miss going to Church. I'd like to, but I don't know where to go. I don't buy into all the dogmatic aspects, but I like the idea of people coming together for some spiritual enrichment or enlightenment or even just to say 'hi' once a week."[12]

The Ghost of Tom Joad was recorded about a decade after *Nebraska.* It is a closely related cousin; acoustic songs tell the stories of those in all kinds of desperate scenarios. Though many of the stories are just as bleak and desolate as they were on *Nebraska,* there is a different hue to the tales that lie within. In the title track itself, we are *waiting for when the last shall be first and the first shall be last.* Tom leaves as a hero, near savior, telling his mom that everywhere where someone is fighting for justice or freedom, he will be there in their eyes. It is a Christlike incarnation. Again like *Human Touch* and *Lucky Town*, we find a more New Testament disposition to the God that regularly shows up. Parenthood and marriage seem to have affected the twists and turns of decision making that the characters make in what are essentially little novelettes. Live, he would speak about how having kids brought a new front line of protection; as he introduced "Sinaloa Cowboys" and "Bilboa Park," he was a father in gut-wrenching emotion looking at what happens to other people's children.

The album's conclusion found in "Galveston Bay" would never have had a chance to happen in *Nebraska.* In *Songs,* Springsteen writes, "I had already written 'Across the Border' a song that was like a prayer or dream you have the night before you're going to take a dangerous journey. The singer seeks out a home where his love will be rewarded, his faith restored, where a tenuous peace and hope may exist. With "Galveston Bay" I had to make these ideas feel attainable. The song asks the question, is the most political act an individual one, something that happens in the dark, in the quiet, when someone makes a particular decision that effects the immediate world? I wanted a character who is driven to do the wrong thing, but does not. He instinctively refuses to add to the violence in the world around him. With great difficulty and against his own grain he transcends his circumstances.

He finds strength and grace to save himself and the part of the world he touches."[13]

Prayer has become a surprisingly common word in Bruce Springsteen's vocabulary. That indeed is how he has been introducing "Land Of Hope And Dreams." Then there was the prayer that he sang at the telethon for the victims of September 11. Remarkably, "My City Of Ruins" had been written almost a year before that dreadful New York morning, but how it perfectly expressed the moment and the seeking of some eternal explanation. Married to U2's worshipful ending to "Walk On," it brought a real sense of all that is best about church into the midst of the event. "My City Of Ruins" would be the closing track on Springsteen's next album, *The Rising*, which would be his most commercially successful work in many long years. As he and U2 succeeded in doing at the Telethon, the album is full of hope and light in the midst of the most despairing and darkest time. Springsteen does not overstep the mark by telling the mourners to catch a grip and look at the bright side of life. It is a remarkable juxtaposition of sadness and joy, doubt and faith, death and resurrection. In that way the spirit has religious connotations in mining the day for belief, but there are also specific pointers to God and transcendent hope.

The Rising was a pastoral response to September 11, the other side of the coin from Steve Earle's political comment on the same. It is likely that Bruce will get around to some of that in these next few years, but for now it was important for him to sooth souls. In the midst of the E Streets Band's first studio outing in fifteen years, it must have been difficult to take the joy of the tour that was sure to fuel a celebratory big music sound and add to the pain of New York's grief. So, while there is the foot stomping stadium strut of "Counting On A Miracle" and the traditional rock bluster of "Further On Up The Road" and "Lonesome Day," the songs of loss are much more in keeping with the sound of "Streets Of Philadelphia."

"You're Missing," "Into The Fire," and "Empty Sky" get inside the souls of the grieving. Springsteen tells the story of so many New Yorkers, and every little angle is enlightening and in some ways healing. From this place of empathy he never leaves them wallowing in the tears that he helps them cry, but brings faith and hope and dreams of that resurrection day, where the album gets its name.

A question that needs to be asked is specifically where does Springsteen see grace and hope and faith and salvation emanating from? Are Patti and his children the avenue toward God, or are they a means in themselves? There seems to be no chance whatever that we will ever have a Damascus Road, evangelical Christian conversion story with all the liturgy that evangelicalism has put into that package. Where Bruce is in that prodigal son story is for all of us to speculate. Wherever he is though, he is going to take us with him. If we go back to the monologue at the start of this chapter, he is connecting with his audience to the extent of inviting them on board his journey and inviting himself on board theirs. In a recent benefit gig for *Double Take* magazine, he gave the audience his product guarantee, "The artist's promise to his audience and the challenge he throws out to his audience which is if I'm going, then you're coming with me."

So off we go further down the Springsteen turnpike toward this land of hope and dreams. If you're a saint or a sinner, a loser or a winner, a whore or a gambler ... whoever you are, whatever you've done ... do not fear, because this land is not about our lack of mistakes or the perfect holiness of our lives. In this land, he says on "Land Of Hope And Dreams," "faith will be rewarded."

TEN

SELF EVIDENT

I n the world of arts, musicians have an unfair disadvantage. If you are a painter or a sculptor, the worth of your piece is not dependent on how many you sell. Apart from prints, there is only one to sell. It is not even dependent on how many people come through the exhibition or gallery, though a huge number of people interested in your work will no doubt give you an advantage. Even with the playwright, the poet, and the novelist, though sales of tickets or books are important, there is not the same demands for commercial success as there is on those who find their gifts and vocation reside in the world that we call very loosely rock 'n' roll.

For some unknown reason, I have found myself involved with a wide variety of singers, songwriters, and bands. Without playing a chord myself, I have spent the last ten years of my life in communities of musicians. My connection is not just friendship. Somehow again by serendipity, a cosmic joke, or by some higher design, I find myself in cafés, my living room, or on the telephone giving advice on all kinds of areas of the business from how good the lyrics are to what record deal to sign. Do not ask me why. I have no idea. Indeed, sometimes after I have left a conversation, I look back and wonder where the advice I gave came from. I have laughed with many friends that it is the closest a Presbyterian like me gets to speaking in tongues.

One of the issues that so often comes up is the sense of worth a singer can have in their work if it is not selling in big numbers. Beyond that, there are those friends who are selling in very respectable numbers who somehow are trapped in a strange and perpetual need to sell more. For example, if the second album sells 40,000 copies but the first sold 80,000, it is deemed a failure and therefore an inferior work. However, if the first one had sold 40,000 and the second 80,000, both would be deemed successful. Then there are the ones who tell me that they cannot get a deal, so they are going to quit. The ability to make musical art is very much chained to the commercial payback in a way an artist or poet's work is not.

Then there is the industry. I have friends who have spent years of their lives and many thousands of dollars making albums that never see the light of day, but are set on some record company shelf somewhere. They have been signed by an A&R man who has been very into their work, but during the recording process, he/she moves on and is replaced by someone who has their own baby, and my mate's album will never get to my CD player. They need to start all over again, if they have the strength of character to come back for more. Then there are those who spend years on some songs, and when the record released, they are so low down in the record company's priority list that month that they disappear into the midst of the industry's infrastructure, and vocations are

down the drain. It is a tough business, and it sadly has less
to do with music and art than cash tills and the whim of
businessmen, rather than those who want to buy CDs.

In such an industry, there is simply nobody like Ani DiFranco.
In spirit, she is a descendent of Woody Guthrie, but at the
same time, she shows traces of English punk queen Soiuxsie
Sioux. As well as those influences from the past, she is
completely contemporary with her tattoo across her chest
and that crusty-like hair. She is scary and gorgeous at the
same time. And she is, without any question of doubt, her
own person. She has stood with the gay community no matter
what the straights said, and then she fell in love with a man
no matter what the gay community said. She has spoken
out about the government and the capitalist system and gun
control and just about anything that gets in her cerebral way.
She does it with power and a deep-seated conviction, but she
also has the humility to admit her imperfections, flaws, and
mistakes, and she never takes herself too seriously.

If any artist today has the right to take her achievements
artistically, commercially, and politically seriously, it is Ani
DiFranco. She was named by VH1 in the 100 Greatest Women
Of Rock 'n' Roll, has been nominated for four Grammy
Awards, and sells a quarter of a million units per release—of
which there have been an amazing fifteen in ten years—and
though we are counting two double live albums, we are not
counting EPs of varying sorts or collaborations with Utah
Phillips. Amazingly, she has just turned thirty-two.

More remarkably and maybe her most prophetic statement
is not so much the canon of her songs, but the way that she
has put her songs into the public domain. She has given an
alternative way. She has bypassed the demons of commerce,
and her radical approach to the industry, which of course is
an outworking of her radical approach to almost every issue
imaginable, is also a model for all kinds of issues that we need

to deal with in a society that has gotten lost in worship of the golden calf.

At the tender age of twenty, out of the necessity of demand for her product and her radical philosophy to put "music before rock stardom and ideology before profit," Ms. DiFranco started Righteous Babe Records.[1] She started the commercial end of her career selling cassettes out of the back of her car after gigs as she trailed the States doing something like 200 concerts a year and mostly traveling and playing alone. As a following started to gather some momentum, the record companies started to come calling. Rather than bow the knee to compromise her art and sell her soul to play the lottery that is the conglomerate world of the record business, DiFranco took the decision to just keep doing as she was doing. She would do it herself and sell it at gigs and through whatever outlets she could. By 1993, she had Scot Fisher on board, a man who sacrificed the big bucks of his legal career to buy a fax machine, through which he launched a record label that ten years later has grown to two coffee pots and a staff of about fifteen.

The grassroots ideology did not stop there. DiFranco decided that instead of the more obvious location of New York City, she would relocate Righteous Babe Records to her home city of Buffalo and take up offices downtown to give some energy to an inner city that was losing its soul. As the late 1990s and early 2000s would see people on the streets of the world stating concerns with the monsters of globalization and large corporations taking over the world, DiFranco did not just march and shout. She did not just sing a radical and alternative agenda; she put her money, or rather initially her friend's money, where her mouth was and gave a model to anyone asking how to resist the over indulgence of capitalism. Righteous Babe Records does not see profit as the bottom line, but art, and more than art, people and neighborhoods.

What a shame that the Church did not show a lead, but instead pretty much mirror-imaged the world in the establishment of a music industry with all the same hallmarks. The Christian music scene has some very particular rules about subject matter and theological correctness. The number of mentions of Jesus per minute is seen as important to the legitimacy of Christianizing the product. How sad then that when it comes to the promotion of artists, the same profit margin seems more important than people, sales needing to exceed certain substantial figures before someone's art is seen as worthy of another album. The same seductive album covers of good-looking girls is important, and the blatant targeting of mass markets is equally dubious ethically. The world is in need of an alternative, and where you would expect it, the opportunity is ignored, and an artist that the Church might point the finger at for being a gay icon even though she is happily married is the rock that cries out in their stead!

From the foundation of an ethically upright business scenario, DiFranco uses her music to make some acerbic observations on American life. One of her most remarkable outbursts across a whole range of issues was written in the wake of the 9/11 tragedy. It would appear on the live collection *So Much Shouting, So Much Laughter* and is a marvelous showcase of her gentle poetic ability and her political rage. It is also a remarkable piece of writing in that in its nine minutes, there are a wide range of emotions to the World Trade Center horror. Beginning with an image of humans as having been reduced to poems that are 90 percent metaphor, she rants and raves, before drawing back to the 3,000-plus victims of 9/11 being more than poems and how we have to make sure that their death is not in vain.

It is important to point out this ultimate sympathy for the victims, because many might feel that elsewhere she is being disrespectful. Of course, she never is, but sensitivities can leave perspective delicate in such an emotional situation. There is a passing compliment to the perpetrators in that by diminishing the people they were about to murder to poetic metaphor, they out-Hollywooded the special effects of blockbuster movies and surpassed news reporters who were left lost for any kind of words to describe an act both vicious but tragically very clever. The sensitivities of the time forbade anyone to make comments on such a perfectly planned and dramatic statement that Al Qaeda made on that fateful day. If Di Franco is going to be so raw in her honesty, we can be sure there is more to come.

So, she asks questions about their poem. Why? Into the beauty of a September New York day, she throws out the accusation that it was America whose "strutting" in all corners of the world that caused itself to suffer such a horror. Like country artist Steve Earle, who got into a lot of trouble with his song about American John Walker Linde, the young man who turned his back on the American dream that he was born into and joined the Taliban, DiFranco wants to know why people would do this to her people, and her answer is in the title of the song "Self Evident," it is what her people have been doing to other people. We are reaping what we have sown.

It is hard to be self-critical at times of such vulnerability and pain. The American people came together in communal ways the like of which had not been seen in many a long year. The genuinely heroic self sacrifice of the fire fighters became a catalyst for strength of character that was admired throughout the world. It had been a long time since America had had such sympathy from either within or without. The rock community is a case in point. Many artists who would have been the first to criticize America in their work were participating in fundraisers and tribute concerts. Less than eighteen months later, however, the war in Iraq had divided the nation and seen world opinion turned around once more.

The rock world too started to speak out in opposition.

Rather than use the time of mourning and renewed sense
of nationhood to reassess, America would simply take the
very actions that had caused the hijacking of the planes in
the first place. Let us not look into our own dark corners and
put our own souls in order. No, we will just go out there and
police the world and as DiFranco would put it "perpetuate
retribution." The lessons we need to learn about ourselves
can be ignored as we go "armed to the teeth" ("To The
Teeth") to teach everybody else a lesson.

Somehow arrogance got there ahead of contrition. In church,
the week after the event, I read this prayer. It is my "Self
Evident," though I am more in a state of questioning than
raging out answers like DiFranco does.

Lord we have watched the special effects
Not of Hollywood
But of evil dressed up in some political or religious cause
Fact and fiction have been blurred before our eyes
We have been drawn in like a good movie plot
Wanting to see what will happen next
Almost wanting something to happen next
Even though we don't want anything else to happen
We have mourned for the victims without dilemma
We have cursed the terrorists without dilemma

But Lord there are many dilemmas
The dilemma of the difference between justice and vengeance
The dilemma of how to love our enemies as Jesus commanded
And the ridding the world of the demonic evil of terrorism
The dilemma of knowing who is perfect enough to fire the first
missile in judgment

So Lord tonight without being sure what to pray
We pray for your mercy

God visit us, whether we are in New York, Kabul or Belfast city
Send your mercy to sort out the pain and hurt and confusion
and fear and discord

So Lord we seek your comfort
For those who have lost loved ones
Fathers, mothers, husbands, wives, sons and daughters, friends
and work colleagues
Lord Jesus called the Holy Spirit the Comforter
We pray it might be so Lord

And Lord we pray for freedom
Freedom from fear and uncertainty
Free from the threats of the devil's stare and his killing and
destruction

So Lord we pray for discernment
For those who are making decisions that affect us all
For those who are making decisions on our behalf
Those who tonight have the people of Afghanistan in their
hands
Give them sensitivity and humanity and Christlike thinking in
their response
As they walk that thin line between justice and vengeance

So Lord we pray for wisdom in our self criticism
We pray for your Spirit's conviction in our soul searching
As we investigate the motives of our hearts
Towards those who are not defined to be as free and civilized
as us.
May we look at our own history
And see where we have been the aggressor and the terrorist
Whether Americans and the attempt to obliterate the native
people
And their current plight on barren and impoverished
Reservations
Or the British crusading in the name of God

Against people all around the world
And here in Ulster where most of us sit today
Because our ancestors took this land by violent acts against the
innocent
May we see our own sinfulness as we point our fingers self
righteously at others
May we seek your forgiveness

Lord we pray for a miracle
Peace
When peace seems impossible
Lord we pray for you to rend the heavens and come down
among us.

In Jesus' name
The Lamb of God who took away the sins of America, Britain,
and Afghanistan and the world we pray
AMEN[2]

When we pray for God to rend the heavens and come down, we must be sure that we want a response. There was a line once in the *X-Files*. Freak of the week was giving Mulder a hard time in the depths of the earth, and in the dialogue he uttered profundity, "Mulder, your problem is that you are still petitioning heaven for answers. What would happen if heaven gave you an answer?" Answers from heaven will not be written by the one who prays, and to seek God to come into the midst of a 9/11 would mean going under the surgeon's knife on his operating table to rid us of all the wicked ways that caused the trouble to begin with, but will certainly need to be cut out if we are to avoid more trouble in seeking a way out. He will not give easy ways out. It costs His people to be part of the answer to their prayers.

DiFranco lists the wicked ways of America in a way that leaves a word like acerbic sounding anaemic and frail. Her three main gripes are the legality of Bush's presidency, the integrity of America's democracy and the media being used as propaganda rather than truth. She makes Steve Earle sound like a Republican! The first is obviously a dig at the blurred election victory, and she has a go at Bush's brother Jeb, too, but the others are tied up in what DiFranco really sees as the sin of the nation; profit as the bottom line. It is that profit line that DiFranco sees as the antichrist. She spells it out in the song "Your Next Bold Move" from her 2001 double album set *Revelling: Reckoning* where she sings about capitalism murdering democracy. The multinationals are the guilty.

She brings in environmental issues and advocates a boycott of the planes and a return to the train (I wonder if the DiFrancos of a century earlier were suggesting we boycott the trains to walk or ride bicycles!) in ways that would have made many an advertiser for trains very proud indeed. She is out for the oil companies, which she would see as those who take away the democracy from America in that the feeling is that on Capital Hill, the oil companies do more than influence decisions. It is interesting that when the Iraqi war came around, those same oil companies would be accused of being the reason a war was fought. The treatment of those counseling girls on abortion issues, those who live on Indian reservations, those on death row, and the peoples of Palestine, Afghanistan, Iraq, and El Salvador are all raised. A woman's rights to choose, and beyond that to simply women's rights, and the death penalty have been big issues in DiFranco's work and life.

It cannot be easy to be involved in an industry where the artist is caught in a dilemma between art and profit margins. It is not only in the ethic of your product and those who create it and sell it that you have to be careful. The way you treat the public is crucial too. There is a subtle but quantifiable difference between getting your product out to those who want it and conning people into buying what they do not really want to stuff your bank balance.

I remember watching a documentary about the sales
campaign behind Meat Loaf's *Bat Out Of Hell 2*. We were
shown over 100 people who strategized a campaign to sell that
album over fifteen years after the original. The target audience
was those who bought it first time around. From there the
choice of first single, cover art, billboards to place ads, and
the newspapers to garner interviews were carefully chosen
in order to give the unsuspecting the same feeling they had
when they first heard *Bat Out Of Hell*. It was a carefully
orchestrated campaign. I was one of the suckers. I loved *Bat
Out Of Hell*. I listened to it over and over and over. Of course
I wanted volume two. Yet, when I had spent the money and
brought it home, I realized that I was a very different person
as a thirty-two-year-old than I had been at sixteen. My tastes
had changed. I was glad I was not necking with the same girl
(actually there was no girl!) and wearing the same clothes
(though I probably was!) and pursuing the same career. I was
certainly not listening to Jim Steinman's big bombastic sound
anymore, but the suits in the offices did not care; they had
my money. It is the same with every product or service we
now buy or receive. Rarely and certainly almost never with
conglomerates or multinationals is there any concern for
people's needs.

The greatest obscenity of such a situation became clear to me
when I was watching another BBC television documentary on
AIDS drugs. I spent some time in South Africa to listen to and
meet with those who have AIDS or are caring for members
of their families with AIDS or are doctors working with those
who have AIDS. A church I attend in Guguletu has an AIDS
testimony every Sunday. I have personal emotions about
the plight in sub-Sahara Africa and the pandemic they are
suffering. So this documentary had my attention. When it
came to why the American government was not encouraging
their drug companies to look at the patent laws that would
allow cheaper drugs to be produced to alleviate suffering and
prolong life of the people in my beloved Cape Town and the

rest of sub-Sahara Africa, the answer was that the loss of profit would discourage the drug companies from producing the drugs. So why do people make drugs? Is it to help the sick or alleviate a human catastrophe? No—to make profit! The good idea of free trade has been so diseased that there might be no drug to save us from its rampant killing of our souls. Truly Jesus was right when He warned that we could not serve both God and money, that it profits us nothing as individuals or nations when we gain the world and lose our souls.[3]

DiFranco has to live with those tensions. Being an independent record company executive, she does not have the temptation of huge advertising budgets, and although she is garnering a higher profile in the media, it is probably by seeing her live or by word of mouth that someone will buy her work. Sting said at a recent awards ceremony that "the art itself is your reward." Though that must be easier for a millionaire rock star to philosophize it is profound wisdom for the songwriter who is being exploited by the industry. DiFranco is confident that her art is her vocation and the need for sales is secondary, maybe even further down the priority list, behind the many causes she passionately believes in. And yet, she has to live, to fund her little cottage industry. She now has to continue the revolution by getting her work out to those who want it and respecting those who do not want it enough to refrain from capitalist sin.

ELEVEN

EXODUS

Redemption songs are in the air, blasting out from speakers perched precariously on the top of a nearby shack. The streets for some distance around are hearing what can only be described as their most perfect soundtrack. If ever a sound fitted a place, it is reggae on a township. As Bob Marley's "Exodus" hurtles towards me, it mingles with these thoughts in my head, feelings in my heart, and urges in my soul. It is a song of liberation. It is a song whose rhythms believe the words. It is a song that smiles in the midst of so many reasons to hang your head. It is a song that raises people up, lifts their spirits toward God, and asks for a similar salvation that the children of Israel experienced all those centuries past. It is a skankingly good township jive, and the urge almost bursts my soul.

It is a warm winter South African morning, and I am alone, walking casually down Dada Street, wondering how on earth I got here, and my broad smile gives away the ecstasy of the epiphany in my soul. "Malo," I say to those I meet along the road. It is the only word (apart from Bafana, Bafana! the colloquialism for the nation's soccer team) that I know in their language. It is enough to feel the deepest sense of connection. I am in the Khayelitsha township on the outskirts of Cape Town, where my skin would have been a crime big enough to hand me down an execution just over a decade before. Indeed, it is a place that most of the white South Africans I meet tell me I need security still. Luckily, indeed blessedly, for me, I know these streets a lot better than they do even though I have come 6,000 miles to walk them. As I walk, feeling as happily content as any time in my entire life, I ponder on the miracle of this place and the history of the South African nation and the joy of feeling a part of it. I toss up a prayer that that miracle might continue as these people who I have come to love with all of my heart fight the enemies of the shack, poverty, and now HIV/AIDS.

Bob Marley grew up in Kingstown, Jamaica, and was conditioned in similar conditions to the Xhosa people who have migrated to the Western Cape. To be fair, his shanty, Trenchtown, in the '50s would have made this suburb of Khayelitscha known as Harare seem like Movie Star Avenue in Beverly Hills, but it would have had the same sense of poverty, oppression, and alienation from the white wealth not very far down the track. The picture would be the same too, the mosaic of packing case wood and rusting corrugated iron houses, the debris across the road, the car tire as a sought after toy, the scrawny chickens wandering aimlessly, and the shoe on a string hanging over a telegraph wire. Around the corners of the patchwork walls lurks all kinds of township violence. It was from the shanty neighborhood of Trenchtown that Bob Marley married his political grievance with Rastafarian religion and that reggae rhythm to become the third world's first international superstar.

Time magazine called him the most influential musician of the second half of the twentieth century. He is arguably the most religiously inclined songwriter in rock history. Some might point to George Harrison's Krishna conscience or Bono's Christian influences, but for those two artists, their faith was a central part to their lives, and that came through in their work. Marley was a missionary with an evangelical zeal that made him Rastafarianism's most effective prophet. He was the man who did with his faith what he did with his musical genre—he took them from the backwaters of a government yard in Trenchtown and made them global. He is the only artist I am looking at in this book who is genuinely acknowledged as a prophet.

Marley's albums are as up-front in their religious evangelical zeal as anything coming out of the contemporary Christian music industry; there are as many biblical references, prayers, and worship to God and warnings against the devil as anything coming out of that genre. Yet, Marley evades the derision that is targeted at so many artists who sing of the Christian faith and more than that becomes a rock icon as much as he is revered as a Rastafarian prophet. At the outset of his live album, *Babylon By Bus*, he introduces the gig "Greetings in the name of his Majesty Emperor Haile Selassie I, Jah, Rasti Fari, Ever living, ever fearful, ever sure Selassie I the first." As many Christian artists dip below the radar of their faith to avoid being stereotyped, Marley had to make no apologies. As reviewers slam Christian artists for singing about things that are irrelevant to those without a belief in Jesus, so Marley was rarely accused.

Could it have been something to do with the fact that Rastifarianism wins all cool and credibility battles with caricatured Christianity? Let us compare and contrast. Theologically there are differences, but Jesus, the Bible, and an afterlife of salvation or damnation are all fundamental to both. Rastifarians do add the divinity of Haile Selassie, but that might be neither cool to the pagan nor the Christian. Where Rastas take the war is in the cultural and behavioral patterns of the holy man life!

First there is the hair. For the caricature Christian boy, there is short back and sides with a Republican parting! For the Rasta Man, you get dreads, natty dreads if you like, the coolest hairstyle any man can ever wear! In many of the caricature Christian churches, there are seventeenth century hymnal dirges, or in the more up to date, saccharine little choruses lost in their own little worship industry alleyway. For the Rasta Man, the great prophet Marley writes about "Jamming in the name of the Lord" and a "Rasta Man Vibration Yeah! Positive." Then of course there is the behavior. The caricature Christian cannot smoke, drink, and swear, where the Rasta Man gets to smoke marijuana spliffs as a sacrament! The caricature Christian has even had the symbol of wine that Jesus used for His most precious and powerful blood, the centerpiece of their faith replaced by some diluted watered down version, sadly maybe a more relevant symbol! So we are on a loser there. One thing Bob Marley certainly had was cool, according to society's standards.

It is the theological part that has probably hindered him being the greatest evangelist of any religion to the youth of the latter part of the twentieth century. Much as Rastafarianism seems attractive and tempting, believing that an Ethiopian Emperor who will not go down in history as a kind or godly leader of his people is to be believed in and worshiped as another incarnation of Jesus is a little too far fetched. Before those of us with an orthodox Christian faith have a snigger, maybe it is good to remember that maybe our own beliefs in someone creating the world, partings seas to let Israelites through, a virgin birth, five thousand fed with a few fish and loaves, a dead man raised to life, moving a huge stone in front of His tomb and wandering around meeting His disciples with holes in His hands, side, and feet leaves a few chasms of faith jumps, too! We who build our beliefs on supernatural acts should be the last to point fingers at others, no matter how deluded we feel that they might be!

Rastafarianism blossomed in the Kingston ghettos much better than any kind of green vegetation would. Actually its main prophet before Marley was born eighty miles from Kingston in the same parish of St. Anns where Marley was born. Marcus Garvey was a man on a mission to make the black man's lot much better. It had a very pragmatic side before the spiritual kicked in. He founded the United Negro Improvement Association and would encourage the black person to look to Africa for the fulfilment of Old Testament prophecy. It was not long before he got the event that seemed to fulfill his prophecy. When Haile Selassie was crowned the Emperor of Ethiopia, Garvey had his Messiah. Building quickly on these events was a theology that saw the return from exile of the black Diaspora to their African homeland.

Selassie's divinity was something that Marley was evangelistic about. In her book, *An Intimate Portrait By His Mother*, Cedella Booker writes about her conversion to Selassie's divinity: "Nesta taught me the divinity of Haile Selassie I, Emperor of Ethiopia and most holy son of Jah, who walked the earth like a humble and ordinary man but he was the living and true godhead in the flesh. Nesta taught me that Haile Selassie was descended from the tribe of David and the seed of Jesse, that his great-ancestor was Solomon, that he was the living presence of Jah among men."[1] Selassie however never claimed such a place in God's redemptive plan and was very uneasy when he arrived for a visit to Jamaica and found the dreadlocked masses revering him, much as the apostle Paul and Barnabas were aghast to be hailed as gods during a missionary stop off in Lystra.

Slavery has been with us since time immemorial, but in the nineteenth century with the driving force of Christians, it had been near obliterated. Still Marley reminded us on "Slave Driver" that people can be said to be free in theoretical terms but still practically bound in their poverty. The law may have set them free, but the system was still a gaoler, meaning that in practice the former black slaves had little chance in the free market system to rise above the squalid conditions of the ghetto. If it brought less guilt to the former white slave drivers, it certainly did not remove their culpability in the perpetration of the merciless conditions in which their fellow human beings had to live.

Though Christians were the instigators, thank God, in the demolition of slavery, the white churches were not doing an awful lot to alleviate the pitiful conditions of Trenchtown. It may have been a reason why Marcus Garvey was forced to look elsewhere for redemption. With a need for transcendent hope and finding the church as complicit in the Babylonian despair, Garvey created a system of belief that gave the necessary spiritual backbone of aspiration needed to amass a common purpose and energize the defiance.

Marley is critical of the Christian Church in several songs, most notably on "Get Up Stand Up," where he attacks the preachers who distract the people with the hope of heaven while they live in hell on earth. His grievance is not with Jesus, but with those who oppress or fail to liberate in Jesus' name. This has been a sad trait of evangelical Christianity for some time. While the soul is seen as more important than the body and the soul's eternal condition more crucial than the body's living conditions, Jesus' words about God's will and kingdom on earth as it is in heaven somehow get missed.

When the former South African President FW De Klerk met with my students in Cape Town in 2002, he suggested that all the National Party had done in the late '40s was to institutionalize what was happening in reality through the rest of the world. It was no excuse and does not diminish the blame, but it is a fact. It can work the other way around also. You can rid the world if institutional slavery without ever dealing with the unwritten color codes and oppressive systems.

Christianity has had a marvelous ability to dismiss anything for which an opposing ideology or faith view stands. It has thus been able to ignore the socialism of the New Testament, where those who had given to those who had not, targeting Marxism, and therefore everything Marx stood for was wrong. Care for the poor in any practical way can therefore be dismissed as Marxist, and anyone involved in the overthrow of the injustices of the system that causes poverty can very quickly be labeled Communist and is marginalized, ostracized, and vehemently opposed. The poor can then be left in their ghettos and their defiance stood up to as some evil criminal force. Or apartheid can be supported as a morally strong political system in South Africa because Nelson Mandela was found guilty of terrorist charges. The evil that led him to armed struggle is ignored, upheld, and supported.

Rastifarianism is all about a salvation that will come on the very earth that we know. The belief that Marcus Garvey instituted was that a king would come to Africa to bring the exiles in Jamaican Babylon home. The Rastas believe Ethiopia to be of biblical significance, the place to where God's chosen fled. From this there was a short distance to go to create the belief of a literal return to an Ethiopian Promised Land. It was the title track of perhaps Marley's greatest work— *Exodus–Movement of Jah People.*

There are many questions for the heathen bald heads to ask of this sojourn to the land of milk and honey. Just a few years

141 | ELEVEN

after Marley's death, Ethiopia would again be center stage in the world of rock when every existing superstar with a few exceptions would perform at Live Aid to try and deal with the catastrophic famine of Marley's Promised Land. It would take a lot more than a few ships to transport Afro Jamaicans back to Ethiopia to release them from the cycle of poverty; indeed, such ships might lead them into even more dire consequences.

Not that we should dismiss Marley's chant in "Exodus": *Set the captives free.* There are issues of slavery and racism and Marley's concept of Babylon that need a serious look. In some ways, what Marley did for racism was to eliminate it by the love of the music. In the mid-'70s, most pop and rock music was divided into color codes, but Marley crusaded across the lines and gained respect and fandom from both whites and blacks. Maybe the head of Island Records, Chris Blackwell, deserves more credit for that than Marley. Blackwell was a Jamaican and wanted to break the reggae sound across the world for many more reasons than just financial. So he took the original mixes of "Catch A Fire" and added rock guitar himself. It sent reggae global, and it would not be long before three white boys with the name of Marley's Trenchtown enemies, The Police, would be making white reggae rock!

Chris Blackwell is one of the various white people who played an important role in Marley's life. His dad, of course, was a white man who married Bob's mother, but then took off in his own exodus. Later he would have an affair and the obligatory child with Jamaica's Miss World Cindy Breakspeare, known to Rita Marley as "white woman." Blackwell is Jamaican by birth. As head of Island Records, he had a reputation for putting artistic freedom and integrity before sales. He would have a roster that included John Martyn and later U2. He was a true musical visionary, but he was also a shrewd businessman. He was for the freedom of art first, but that did not mean ignoring the sales figures. He had the vision to break Marley into mainstream rock status. This clarifies rather than blurs Marley's understanding of Babylon not being just white people per se. Some have suggested a hypocrisy that Rastafarianism is an anti-white black-only religion, but this is simply a generalized outcome of some of its genuine beliefs. Ethiopia was holy Mount Zion, and the white system from where they were fleeing was Babylon. In very general terms of course, Babylon was a white man's system. It was the white man who had created the powers of the Western world and its decadent technological prison. In doing so, the white man was to blame for the dispersion of the African people and so many ending up in the townships of Jamaica. Yes, the white man was to blame for Babylon, but he was not outside the scope of salvation. When a journalist asked Marley what he needed to do to become a Rasta, he did not reply grow dreads, change the color of your skin, and smoke ganga; he said, "You must start by being born again."[2] It was an open invitation. The ganga was not a necessity for salvation anymore than being baptized is within most evangelical Christian churches.

In many ways Marley's reggae was the old freedom essence of black gospel to a political back beat. It had political defiance, and, though not as detailed in the telling, was full of news reportage and opinion, but then added that transcendent and joyful hope of the old black slave songs that believed God would set them free. In "Them Belly Full," he spells out the injustices and stark inequality and then calls on the hungry to escape their troubles and sickness by dancing, I guess like their jamming, in the name of the Lord. It might sound like escapism or an ignoring of the plight, but the music they are dancing to is Jah music, and for the Rasta, music sustains the soul. Music in the Rasta faith community, as indeed it was for the black Christian slaves, is a theological practice, a creed proclaiming medium on a power with the sermon. Jesus said, "Man shall not live by bread alone but by

every word that proceeds from the mouth of God." Dancing
to Jah music here has a liturgical quality to feed the soul
to help deal with a starving body. The white oppressors of
Babylon should realize the limitations of bread alone and
give as much attention to the alleviation of poverty as to the
accumulation of capitalist wealth.

See too the ecstatic spiritual worship of jamming. This was
liberation theology on the streets. As many professors
in theological seminaries and political leaders in South
America debated the pros and cons of Liberation Theology,
Marley took it from the streets of the poor to the stages of
the world. When evangelical theologians critique Liberation
Theology, they may well recognize the strength of its tenets
in compassionate action for the poor. However, there is
suspicion of it as siding too much with the poor, to the extent
indeed that the voice of God is the voice of the poor. There is
also a suspicion that loving your neighbor becomes equated
with loving God. This seems a simplistic definition, and again,
when they can disagree in doctrinal definitions, they can
ignore the more important issue: the poor. When Bono went
into the inner sanctums of the American government, he did
not tell them that more than 2,000 verses in the Bible had
patriarchs, prophets, Jesus, and Paul raging about the purity
of doctrine. He was making the point that though God cannot
be equated with the poor, He has a serious interest in their
well being. Whatever we think of the theology, the liberation
should not be tagged on at the end, but to the fore in all our
decision making.

In the conclusion of his book, *Dread Jesus*, William David
Spencer shows how at least strains within Rastafarianism are
returning to a Christo-centric root of belief. As Haile Selassie
was against his divination and followed Jesus Christ, so some
Rastas are seeing him not as God incarnate but as a Luther-
like figure who pointed them to a new understanding of God.
This would add Rastafarianism to that long list of Christian

denominations. Spencer suggests that their acceptance into that widest view of the Church will bring their critique into necessary dialogue for Christianity. Quoting from Ian Boyne, religious reporter of the *Jamaican Sunday Sun* in 1983, we see how Rastas are returning to Christ: "The Twelve Tribes now accept the entirety of Scripture. They emphasize Jesus of Nazareth and hold that it is through Him that all people must be saved."[2] Return to belief is easier than return to fellowship with the white Christian Church; however, as Boyne goes on, "But members are still alienated from the established church. They usually refer to what they see as the hypocrisy of those Christians who claim to practice love while justifying many forms of oppression or of those who uncritically accept many aspects of Westernization in the name of their faith yet condemn indigenous black forms of expression as un-Christian."[3]

The system that keeps the unchained slaves from being truly free was known as Babylon. The reference to Old Testament exile was a powerful one. As the children of Israel were taken from their homes and were forced to sing the Lord's song in a strange land, Jamaica was a foreign land to the Rastas who now had a belief in the Promised Land of Ethiopia. Babylon was to be resisted at every angle.

I found myself chatting to a Rasta on the Masiphumelele township in Sun Valley outside Cape Town. He was selling fruit as so many of the Rastas do. Indeed, it is reckoned that they keep TB off the townships by their street corner trade. When I asked for a photograph, he stood way back and laughed. He muttered about Babylon and technology, which was hard for a baldhead to appreciate in light of the fact that what made the photograph so cool was the trendiest VW van that you ever saw that doubled up as his shop! When I suggested that the Bob Marley whose photograph he was wearing on his T-shirt was a very photographed man, it seemed to drift past like ganga smoke on the wind. Yet, still, when I shared that we were on the township to make people's lives better and that the evils of Babylon were something Jesus spoke out against, we had a sense of common ground.

I wish I could have contradicted his general impression that white churches maintained the Babylon system rather than being involved with the Rastas in ridding the world of its evils. If our theology in all its over-protected purity fails to ignite a compassionate activism in favor of the oppressed, then is it of any use whatsoever, or would the New Testament writer James be telling us that theology without works is dead?[4] Does it also distract us from the truth of Scripture? In that story of Exodus that became so influential for Bob Marley, God showed that He cares for the oppressed, that His eye is on their plight. He also shows that His concern is more than a passing empathy that will become activated when they understand how to explain Him. He acts on their behalf and then urges them to become involved in their freedom—a freedom of which He becomes an advocate as He becomes a very obvious enemy of their oppressor. So where am I in the Old Testament tale, maintainer of Pharaoh's regime or changing sides with Moses to free the people?

I can believe it or I can make excuses to ignore it by saying, "but what the Bible means by transgression is ... what the truth of the children of Israel's exodus is ... and what Jesus meant by preaching to the poor and setting the prisoners free is ... captivity ..." while the poor continue to live in the hell of earth, or the Babylon, or whatever way your semantics want to more correctly define it!

TWELVE

UNPLUGGED, UNMERITED FAVOR

We are all jugglers. From the moment we are born, we are thrown balls that we spend our lives keeping in the air. When my daughter was born, the first thing I did was count ahead to what Olympic Games would be her first reasonable chance of a gold medal! No pressure! There are many other expectations our parents hurl toward us. Catch! A few years in and we are starting to socialize with peers. Another ball is tossed. Look like this. Act like this. Dress like us. Be cool. If you want to be in our gang ... Catch! There might even be a few balls in there. School flings an academic ball. The Church casts a spiritual one, though it is sadly more likely to be a behavioral code. We go to college with another batch, and our chosen career chucks more and more pressures, and who knows, sporting or artistic ability might pitch yet another. Catch! And there we are, juggling. If we want to be loved,

accepted, affirmed, we must keep them all in the air, and
sometimes they bounce off each other to make it all a mess of
stressful living.

As a university chaplain, I am often asked, "What is the
biggest issue you have to deal with living and working
with students?" I can tell that they are expecting the usual
suspects of sex or drugs or rock 'n' roll, though I imagine if I
said rock 'n' roll, it would be like a confession of the leading
of my own flock astray. Believe me, some of them would
love that self confession! They are a little surprised when I
tell them that the thing I have had to pastor most in the nine
years that I have been living with students is that so many of
them come to me and say,

"Steve, can I talk to you?"

"Yeah, what is it?"

"I don't believe God loves me."

The fact is that this is the greatest yearning of every soul
across the entire world. Our most basic need is to be loved,
to be accepted, to feel that we belong. The second need is so
interconnected with the first that they cannot be separated. It
is security. My students do not want to think that if they wake
up in the morning with a spot on the end of their nose, they
will no longer be loved and accepted.

My students live in a world that is rational, sensible, and
fair; where the first are first, and so it should be. The cool
are affirmed and accepted. The beautiful are sought after.
The talented reach the top. If you are none of these things,
then what are you expecting? A nerd on the front page of the
celebrity magazines? An uncoordinated couch potato on the
all star team? A high school drop-out gaining a scholarship
for a postgraduate doctorate in nuclear physics? Come on!

We would not have it any other way. In the end, it is the fact that it is so rational, sensible and fair that leads to every piece of physical, emotional, psychological, and mental damage that we will suffer as we live out our time on this planet. It is where all our inferiorities and insecurities are given birth and then the nourishment to mature. It is the greatest advertising campaign for alcohol and drugs. It is what causes young men to commit suicide. It is what leads every young woman into eating disorders. It leaves all of us stressed, always trying in vain to impress. It leads to a fakeness and shallowness that is keen to not let people know what we are really like. A rational world leads to many illogical acts to oneself and to others, as human beings constantly struggle to be the first and avoid being the last. We live on a graceless planet. My students are jugglers.

Lauryn Hill would be very clearly among the first one of the beautiful and successful people. Having topped the charts and won Grammys with her band The Fugees, her debut solo album *The Miseducation of Lauryn Hill* garnered no less than ten Grammy nominations and five actual awards. The publicity pushed the sales of the album, which had actually sold more copies than any other female artist ever had in its first week of release, to five platinum disc status.

She is the queen of hip hop, a musical pioneer who has been described by Public Enemy's Chuck D as the "Bob Marley of the twenty-first century." She has even found herself married into the Marley clan as wife of Bob's son Rohan and got to work with Aretha Franklin on her 1999 album *A Rose is Still a Rose*. Growing up in South Orange, New Jersey, where she was born in 1975 and brought up in a devout Methodist home, Hill could never have imagined just how "first" she would be before she was even twenty-five.

On the back of such success, Hill steps out very unself-consciously onto the familiar *MTV* unplugged set and before a small and intimate studio audience suggests in the most certain of terms that being first is not all that it is cracked up to be. In one of the many spoken introductions she confesses, "I had created this public persona, this public illusion ... and it held me hostage ... I couldn't be a real person because you are too afraid you know what your public will say and at that point I had to do some dying and really accept the fact that look this is who I am and I have a right to be who I am and all of us have a right to be who we are and whenever we submit our will ... will is a gift ... it's given to us ... whenever we submit our will to someone else's opinion ... a part of us dies ..." The entire evening is a testimony of how Hill has found God in a new way and how that has allowed her to kill off the "pop star" that she had become to reveal the real Hill that He had created her to be. She even says, "This is the first time you've met me."

The performance became the most remarkable CD and DVD, *MTV Unplugged 2.0*, in more ways than one. That an artist who has set the world literally alight with a work of genius, as many hailed *The Miseducation of Lauryn Hill* to be, to come onstage with just an acoustic guitar and set of almost entirely brand new songs is not the done thing in the world of pop superstardom. Even more amazing is that a company as big as Sony would allow her to do so. At best, most of the songs are bedroom works in progress. At worst, this is an album of so many flaws that a myth could be extinguished in an instant. Here is the newly crowned queen of hip-hop taking on a folk singer persona. Your head goes into sonic culture shock. She's no great guitarist, and sometimes the basic strumming style grates, and the listener is left wishing for a little more musically. How will these sound if they make her next "real" album? She misses notes and is clumsy over many a chord; she stumbles and restarts. It is not the making of a modern big label release.

Set aside for a moment cynicism toward the major record

labels. This was a brave move by Sony. In allowing the warts and all, they allow Hill to conjure a two-CD set that as a happening is unique and powerful and as spiritually deep and prophetic as anything that is sent out from the Big Studios of the Big Music empires. The sum here is much, much greater than all of its parts. Indeed, the parts are in places less than mediocre, but the sum is quite a sensational happening. The songs are almost an aside to the message, and yet there are some powerful lyrical diatribes against third millennium society ills, exposing the sin of hedonism, celebrity, industry, government, commerce, etc. It is prophetic stuff, and though the rapping is what struggles most in the minimalist music, there are some catchy melodies too, and all in all, the entire message is a very gripping thing.

This is the document of a pop idol stripping back her skin to pour the contents of her soul all over a stage, a television, and a pop record. This is the journal you lock away in your drawer being read to the entire world. Hill's songs in progress are actually her soul speaking aloud through her own life in progress. It is almost like a huge cross between a testimony and a sermon where the songs are just nails on which to hang the pictures of her main points that are spoken between, rather than sung in, the songs. There is twenty-five minutes of chat broken into an introduction and seven interludes, and rather than finishing with a big musical crescendo, there is an outro that closes the show with her telling the audience that she is crazy and deranged but at peace.

Throughout, Hill is sharing how she has dealt with her voice, her dress, and her public persona, breaking free from who the world thinks she is and has made her think she is to find herself. She says, "Fantasy is what people want but reality is what they need and I'm just retired from the fantasy part." Without doubt, it is a spiritual exorcism, confession, and recommitment. She speaks about how God has taught her what is wrong and then given her the aids towards a solution.

When she says, "a lot of miracles have happened in a short time," you sense that we are listening to God at work on a life. She breaks down during "I Gotta Find Peace Of Mind" as she cries out in thanks for God's mercy.

The need for God's mercy is highlighted throughout the songs. She has a very clear self-awareness of her human condition; her condition and her need for change. Her understanding of that condition is from a very biblical source. In "Mystery Of Iniquity," she fears those who are deluded and unaware that through Adam the whole of humankind is going to die. The Scriptures begin with Adam and Eve being in connection with God. St. Paul sees their fall as still having consequences for the entire human race, "by the trespass of the one man death reigned through the one man."[1] It is out of this doctrinal belief that Hill feels all the sins she raps and rants against spring from. In a different slant on a similar theme to Radiohead, she does not find the devil so much in big corporations and government, although she does not deny they are there. She is more focused on the effects of this human condition on her life and the interpersonal relationships that make up and break up our social networks.

In "Adam Lives In Theory," Hill takes the Garden of Eden story and brings into it a drama of sexual promiscuity, where Eve allows herself to be seduced in the heat of emotion and height of passion, but finds that the pleasure of a moment leads ultimately to lasting guilt and thus recognition of sin which has consequences in the form of a child, poisoned in the purity of her blood stream and death. She shows how our first two ancestors and all of us who have followed them (she explains in her introduction that Adam represents everyone of us) spend their time making excuses and blaming each other and cleverly uses the idea of safe sex protection as an image for the covering of shame like Adam and Eve in the garden covering their nakedness. In the end she is asking on behalf of all of us what we are going to do about our situation and that in the end we need to look back to the Creator's original intent to be de-conditioned from our conditioning so that we might be re-conditioned to the unconditional love of God.

What Hill is keen to share with those who listen is all about how her heart and soul have been renewed by a whole new mind-set of what the real issues of this life really are. God is acknowledged and given thanks for revealing the truth to her. It would seem that those who are first have the same dilemmas and crisis of living as those who are not first or even who are last. One of Hill's recurring themes is how "everybody's in the same mess ... I'm in a mess and God is dealing with me every day." In the end it is not the position in the game that you are in, which messes you up; it is the game itself. Even if you are way out in front in the game, as Lauryn Hill was, you still don't win in the depth of who you are. When you are first, you have to be continually worried about staying first.

The other half of that verse of St. Paul's in Romans 5 is "how much more will those who receive God's abundant provision of grace and of the gift of righteousness reign in life through the one man, Jesus Christ."[2] There is little doubt that Hill is not so concise in the explanation of this half of the Christian story of grace that seems so central to her message. There is a line about Jesus being crucified, but even that is a cover version of her father-in-law Bob Marley's "So Much Things To Say" and is followed with references to Jamaican heroes Rastafarian guru Marcus Garvey and slave leader Paul Bogle.

Hill is a fascinating marriage of her Methodist roots and her husband's Rastafarian heritage. His natty dreaded presence is felt throughout the show, and he even plays some tom tom percussion in what can only be seen as a Rastafarian celebration on "Conquering Lion." Christians are quick to claim Hill as one of theirs with no reference to the impurities of her Rasta baggage. In other articles and reviews, her Rastafarianism will be highlighted without a single acknowledgement of the Christian thread. Considering this syncretism, her sense of peace in being herself can be drawn from either strand. For the Rasta there is a very powerful confidence found in being black. After years of oppression from the so called superior white race, the Rasta revolution was to create within the black mind-set the belief that they were the people of God. This is a powerful message of self-worth, of being happy as they are, and never being tempted to be somebody else. Rastafarianism gives the black peoples caught in poverty and injustice the pride to believe that they were the people, that they could be happy as they were, not in their conditions, but in their skin.

However, this "doctrine" within the Rasta revolution has much more to do with political salvation than with personal salvation. For the Rasta it is not about being saved from hell and going to heaven. It is about a people in exile being set free from the bonds of slavery and returning home to the land of promise, in their case Ethiopia. Hill's application on this amazing MTV night is a very personal sense of being set free. It is not political freedom that she is talking or singing about here. In the songs, she alludes to deliverance and being lost and then being found and of getting another chance. These are all Christian images of salvation, a salvation that can set you free from your sin, your own self image, and the opinions of others.

Whereas much of mainstream Christianity has an over emphasis on being saved from the penalty of past sins and from the very presence of sin in a heaven of the future, Hill ignores both these aspects of the Gospel to concentrate on being saved from the power of sin in the present. This is a woman who has broken the chains of the power that sin has upon us in the everyday. Yet it is more than just the power of sins committed, but a ripping asunder of the guilty disposition

that Adam and Eve created for man and womankind as
pictorially revealed when Christ died on the cross and the
curtain in the temple that separated worshipers from the Holy
of Holies was rent in two.

This removal of the barrier between humans and God allows
for new relations between the Creator and His created. For
humans there is now an opportunity to know the love of God.
Psychologists would agree that there are basic psychological
needs that all of us share—love, security, and significance.
What one of the world's biggest pop stars is telling us loud
and clear between songs and in the songs of this performance
is that she has met those psychological needs. She is no
longer striving to be loved. She no longer has insecure fears
that hold her hostage to her performance or her appearance.
Her significance is no longer dependent on her playing out
some act. She has found love, security, and significance
outside of where the rest of the world usually seeks for it.
She is free from the expectations of others. God has shown
her that living up to the demands of others is a lie. She puts
it very succinctly and well when she says, "We've been told
to protect our outer man while our inner man is dying."
To invert the wisdom, if you nurture the soul, outward
appearances are not so necessary. Lauryn Hill has dropped
all the balls. She is no longer a juggler. She has caught the one
ball that brings us inner peace, God's grace.

From this place of grace, Lauryn Hill has been able to defeat
the stigmatizing, labeling, grading social system, to live
outside of the fear and stress of such a treadmill. This brings
a peace and calm that literally, as Jesus put it to His disciples,
the world cannot give.[3] This is the message for the world
of pop. It is more rebellious than Marilyn Manson can ever
dream about. It turns all of the unwritten rules of relational
engagement on their head. It changes the world in you and
outside of you. Hill says, "People want fantasy but they need
reality, I've retired from fantasy." The working out of the truth

inside of Hill's heart and soul is the concert she is able to do as a result. The sense of vitality in this salvation of Hill's is infectious and empowering, whereas many Christians continue to be burdened about the fear of sin, even when they believe Jesus has atoned for our sin once and for all when He cried on the cross, "It is finished."[4] Hill gives the clear sense of believing that it is finished and starting a new life of liberation to achieve what can be achieved through God's mercy and strength.

It is always good to ask who are the real rebels in rock—the bands who throw television sets out of their hotel bedrooms, or those who read Bibles at the back of tour buses? It is also important to ask which rock stars pose the most danger to our children? I was watching Vigilantes Of Love, in a Christian music venue on the north coast of Ireland. Normally used to taking their faith-based songs into the club environment, the drummer had even used masking tape to black out a label on his woolly hat that he felt might not be appropriate in such a spiritually sanitized environment. It is not hard to understand why parents would be thrilled to leave their teenage offspring at the door of such a place. "No Swearing" a poster on the wall commands; alcohol is the only piece of décor missing in a building kitted out like many state-of-the-art bars. Here is a wholesome alternative to the pubs and clubs around the area. And the Vigilantes Of Love to boot!

Near the end of the set, my "turning-thirty" mate, who was just there to hear the band, says he is off to the pub down the road to catch the last orders. Then he throws in an extra piece of insight. With a caring rather than a critical spirit he says, "and you know apart from a glass of beer and a fag (cigarette), there is nothing happening down at The Anchor bar that is not happening here." Wow, that put me off the encore! Yet after a night running around my brain, I had to agree and realize how easily we are duped into thinking the most perilous places are safe. What my friend was aware of was the insidious dangers of lust and envy, jealousy, and selfishness. The need to look good to compete with your peers in the conquest of the opposite sex was leaving the room reeking with insecurity, inferiority, hurt, and despair.

When I am asked about the dangers of rock music by parents, youth leaders, teachers, or ministers, I am aware of the risk of a similar false sense of security. Marilyn Manson and Eminem are the easy answer. Avoid the ones who swear, and you now have the benefit of parental guidance stickers to fend off the perpetrators of darkness.

Like our Christian music venue, even the seemingly safest artists can be a danger. Few teenage girls end up with an eating disorder because of the number of times Eminem used the "F" word! Where pop is at its most dangerous might not be in the words at all, but in the image. The dressing up in the goth-like clothes of a Manson is not going to cause a fifteen-year-old boy to shoot down his classmates any more than someone dressing like a golfer is going to start making judgments on who can join their gang!

However, the shapes and figures and complexions and hairstyles that fill the pop pages and album covers can set teenagers and particularly vulnerable girls into fits of inferiority complexes. Perhaps the greatest burden upon our youth and a burden that will lead them into all kinds of frightening scenarios is the slavery of appearance. The social system that is centered around relationship and love and acceptance is the overriding factor in whether we turn into balanced human beings or people with emotional, mental, or spiritual scars, wounds that affect how we live for our own good and for the good of others.

Let us then turn the question on its face. Rather than looking for the dangerous music, let us look for the music that has a positive input into the lives of our teens and let us stop kidding ourselves, into all of our lives. One album that should be recommended to all those who might call seeking advice is Lauryn Hill's *MTV Unplugged 2.0* album. In late 2003, *Rolling Stone* would suggest that *Unplugged* was a "public breakdown" and asks serious questions about Hill's marriage to Marley and worrying suggestions about her relationship with a man named Brother Anthony who they suggest has been her spiritual guru for some time. No matter what the spiritual direction or the state of Hill's mind, the MTV performance is one woman's attempt at eyeballing the repression of our social structures and breaking free from the bondage of the rules and regulations of other people's expectation and opinions. She sings, "I Find It Hard To Say Rebel," but she is about peace of mind and "freedom time," a peace and freedom found in who she is before God and through His mercy, and not what she achieves before others. It is a remarkable message at odds with all that we are conditioned to behave like or believe. Whereas we live in a world that is rational, sensible, and fair, the grace of God is illogical, insane, and totally unfair. A place where the first are last and the last are first. It is a crazy, radical, and revolutionary idea. Totally mad, yet as Lauryn Hill is discovering, it is the only hope that she as a pop star has and all of the rest of us as well.

THIRTEEN

MISERY IS THE RIVER OF THE WORLD

I stepped out past the prostitutes and headed toward the headquarters of my church denomination. The house I was about to move into had been damaged in one of the last bombing of the recent Irish troubles (and no, I was not living there at the time, and no, it was not an everyday occurrence), and I had been relocated to Belfast city center. Without a television, my then girlfriend (now wife) and I would sit on the window ledge and watch Belfast give us a live performance on a Saturday night. It was more exciting than television! A drug drop here, a prostitute pick-up there, and all kinds of goings on everywhere else. You can use that public telephone kiosk at your own risk! So, I got used to the prostitutes congregating at the door of the flats. As I walked away from them this particular morning, I felt a deep desire to connect, say hello, give them a little bit of dignity that society and, this morning, me and my actions withholds from them.

Yet, was this not a good Christian upbringing? Prostitutes are no kind of women for a good Christian boy to be making connections with. Of course it was the exact opposite. As I walked away, I realized that Jesus would have been so comfortable chatting to prostitutes that He would probably have sat down on the steps beside them and forgot about all the so-called business He had to do at the Church House. Befriending prostitutes would have been a higher priority. So as I gazed across all the books I had read, conferences I had attended, and sermons I had heard (and even preached) about following Jesus, I began to ask why I had not been taught how to just pass the time of day with the people Jesus seemed to hang out with.

Tom Waits has spent his career raising the profile of the people who Jesus hung out with and who the Church usually has no time for. Waits' most famous prostitute song is "Christmas Card From a Hooker In Minneapolis." In the form of a note in the seasonal greeting, the story is a happy one. Here is a woman whose world is turning around. She is off the drugs and quit the drink and found a man who will love the baby she is carrying even though it is not his. Sadly, in the last verse, she throws off all pretence and admits there is no man and she needs money to pay a lawyer to get her out of jail. Waits added even more poignancy and sadness to the tale when he played it live by adding "Silent Night" to the beginning. It adds to the possibility of hope but brings reality crashing even more cruelly in the absence of a happy ending.

Waits' work has been founded on the freaks, the outcasts, the most intriguing of the marginalized: prostitutes, strippers, fugitives, hoodlums, criminals, tramps, sewer dwellers, soldiers (mostly war veterans), murderers, arsonists, and the widest variety of drunks imaginable. Where many writers write about themselves or their peers, Waits has a pastor's care for people he sees, writing songs to empathize in many ways with the hope of exorcising their demons. Demons seem to over populate Waits' albums, and the devil himself hangs out, but so does Jesus, maybe not with equal measure, but certainly with equal power. Singing about these characters, bringing them alive in songs, and no doubt exaggerating them for poetic effect may be one of his ways to drive the devil "Way Down in the Hole." Another similarity to Jesus and niggling little jibe at the Church is how Waits loves them no matter what. The grace and the dignity he puts into their lives along with the dime or quarter he drops into their hand is never dependent on "successful" conclusions to their tragedy.

The religious leaders of His day could never quite understand why Jesus would hang out with Tom Waitsian characters. He would often say, "It is not the healthy who need a doctor, but the sick."[1] He would also set a new rule of thumb for our social connections, "Many who are first will be last and the last first."[2] Tom Waits was a "last shall be first" man. There is a marvelous story to illustrate the point that Jay S. Jacob recounts in his biography, *Wild Years*, though he is unable to confirm if it is true or exaggerated. Whether it is true, or like Jesus' story of the prodigal son, which though not true is most definitely true, who cares!

Apparently near the Main Point venue in Philadelphia, there was a restaurant and bar called H.A. Winstons. Taking pride in their classy joint, they would have a lot of the Main Point performers drop by. They wanted Waits, and he would never come. Classy was not his thing. In most cities, he would reside and eat in the wrong side of town, either feeling more comfortable there, or always researching his songs, or both.

One night, Waits turns up at Winstons, and there is great excitement, but Waits walks past the classiness and finds Artie the dishwasher, who he hangs with for an hour washing dishes, ignoring those who were "deserving" of his company. Artie had played somewhere with Waits, and he thought he would hear his story. The dishwasher was the last in the pecking order, and Artie was not liked much, but he was the one Waits connected with at his level to bring him grace and dignity.[1] Jesus did the same one day for a guy named Zaccheus in Jericho. As a tax collector, this little man was as reviled in his day as a drug pusher might be in the neighborhood today. Hated and the last person who deserved time with the day's pop star storyteller, it was he whom Jesus sought out and had dinner with. I wonder if they did the dishes together!

Waits has never been one to sentimentalize the tragic tales he elucidates. There is no sanitizing attempted, and with a voice like his, how could there be? It sounds like the intoxication of tequila with some broken glass from the bottle scraping the back of his throat. It should have a "R" rating. If you let your imagination run wild on how sin as defined in the Old Testament might sound channeled through some computer program that would cough it out as a voice, then you would end up with something that would pretty closely resemble this. It is dark and seamy, welling up in the underground and crawling out like some slithery, slimy monster about to eat up the world. It is rough. It is expressive. And yet it is lovely and addictive and a taste well worth taking the time to acquire. Although for most people it is far too near ugly for the ear's palate, for others it is the most wonderful if not beautiful of sounds. To not acquire it and miss the shadowy wonder of his work and those who populate his songs would be a sad void in your musical experience and indeed theological contemplation. It is rich with realism. It is rich with truth, and it is as honest as any rock voice might ever be. There is nothing like it, like it or not.

Not satisfied with the eccentricity of his voice, Waits has also introduced into the pop and rock idioms the most unlikely orchestra of instrumentation, including artillery shells, old horns, rams' horns, 1929 pneumatic calliope, boomerang seedpods, and hurling that voice through a battery-operated bullhorn. If you were asked to compose the score for the soundtrack of that last hundred-yard walk through the underground tunnels that led to hell, then you would probably come up with the haunting, clanking, dark quirk of staccato percussion and a hotch potch of offbeat sounds that are much too sinister to play when there is a more hopeful destination in mind.

That Tom Waits should have chosen to use that voice as a means to communicate the great fallenness of humanity should be of no surprise. His 2002 release *Blood Money* was an album that could have been used as a musical Ph.D. thesis on the nature of mankind and particularly sin. One particular truth that marinates the rest of the work is the idea that the only thing you can know about mankind is that there "is there is nothing kind about man." No matter what you do to chase out the nature of man, it will always come back to get us.

Blood Money was released on the same day as *Alice* in 2002. From 1993 to 1999, Waits releases nothing, and then in one day we get two! Both albums are songs that Waits had written with his wife Kathleen Brennan for plays directed by avant-garde theater director Robert Wilson. *Alice* was done in 1994 and is based on a relationship between Lewis Carroll and the girl in the looking glass who gives the album its title and has been described by Waits as being about "repression, mental illness and obsessive compulsive behavior."[2] *Blood Money* is a collection of songs from *Woyzeck* written in 1837 by Georg Buchner and to be staged at the Barbican in London in the autumn of 2002. It is the story of a soldier who goes through some crazy medical experiments who discovers that his lover has been unfaithful. All of this contributes to "the descent into madness," and he finally murders his lover. In interviews, Waits would say the songs live outside of the plays, and so they do. It is perfect and familiar terrain for Waits, who has been dealing with people on such margins since his very earliest days. Having said that, "Everything Goes To Hell" is as bleak as even Waits has ever gotten. There is no one else in rock who deals with the darkness in almost the doctrinal discipline of Waits. Yes, we have the Eminems and the Marilyn Mansons, who, to different degrees and with different intended effects, milk the evil of our world, but with Waits it seems to have more of a preacher's intent.

During his obligatory round of radio interviews to promote *Blood Money* and *Alice*, Tom Waits found himself at the mercy of Terry Gross from the *Fresh Air* program on WHYY-FM Radio in Philadelphia. There was a sense that Ms. Gross was no Tom Waits fan. She had done enough research to ask seemingly the right questions, but being able to spar with a character of Waits' dexterity seemed to defeat her. There were moments when she seemed to have Waits on the precipice of the big cosmic questions, and then she reverted to the trivial. Even in Waits there is eventually a vibe of deep dissatisfaction. There is a point in the interview when she is looking for some tabloid sensation and asks Waits, "What's the craziest ride when you were hitchhiking that you would even shudder to think about now?" It is a good question to someone who has been recounting the weird, freaky, and downright scary throughout his career.

Waits however throws a curve. "Well, actually, I had some good things happen to me hitchhiking. I did wind up on New Year's Eve in front of a Pentecostal Church and an old woman named Mrs. Anderson came out. We're stuck in a town with seven people in this town, trying to get out, you know. My buddy was out there for hours and hours, getting colder and colder and it was getting darker and darker and finally she came over and she says, 'Come into the church. It's warm and there's music and you can sit in the back. And we did and they were singing, they had a tambourine, an electric guitar, and a drummer. They were talking in tongues and then they kept gesturing to me and my friend. These are our wayfaring strangers and we felt kinda important. And they took up a collection, they gave us some money, bought us a hotel room and a meal. We got out the next morning. We hit the first ride, seven in the morning and we were gone. It was really nice. I still remember all of that. It gave me a good feeling about traveling."

Cath Carroll begins her book, *Tom Waits*, with the same story, but with a completely different take. In her telling of the same tale she writes, "Mrs. Anderson rather inhospitably began to wave a demonstrative finger at the hapless Waits whenever the spoils of the devil's work were mentioned ... Waits says it gave him a complex and cites this episode as the inspiration for the song 'Down Down Down" from his 1983 album *Swordfishtrombones*."[3] This is Tom Waits too, mining both sides of every story, taking a different take on every life.

Waits' contribution to modern society is that he is constantly bringing before us the characters that we walk past on the street or in the underground without giving a second thought to. Waits does more than give them a second thought; he brings them alive and pushes them through the doors of our living rooms and makes them human in all the wonder of being human without ever daring to clean them up or perfume their marginalized fragrances! He also always reminds us of our human condition. In a world that would attempt to cover up every criminal as a victim of their situation and where we would do the most horrendous of deeds and call it political correctness, Waits lets us know what Jeremiah testified to, that, "The heart is deceitful above all things and beyond cure. Who can understand it?"[4]

Many have tried to ignore such a biblical pronouncement on humanity's condition. Karl Marx was convinced that if the environment was put right, then the heart could be put right. He believed that humans can be put right, but Christians believe in an idea called "original sin," which suggests that every human being is born with that deceitful heart, and until that has been put right, history will never be changed. With the failure of the Marxist influenced communist countries, the indications are that there is something to the Christian analysis. Most communist states would have been damaged within as a result of power mongering, and human beings having an incapacity to act fairly and for the good of all. Something within throws the whole thing off-kilter.

Inside Christianity too, there are those who would try to play down the deceitful heart of mankind. In the latter part of the twentieth century, Matthew Fox, a Dominican priest, was the espouser of a new paradigm on which to build our views on the spiritual wellbeing of humanity. He took issue with the traditional foundation of Christian theology, which is "original sin." This is the idea that as a result of Adam and Eve's sin at the outset of humanity's history and disconnection with God, we are all infected. This is a very difficult thought in light of our contemporary drive to exonerate ourselves from every little casting of blame. It is hard to imagine that the daughter that I marveled at wide-eyed in the moments after her birth has been condemned to some kind of maladjusted condition because of some ancient character or event. The apostle Paul had no doubts of my daughter's sin by association. Her original representatives screwed it up for her. In Romans chapter five, he believes that "sin entered the world through one man"[5] and "by the trespass of the one man, death reigned through the one man."[6] In another letter to the Corinthians, he says, "in Adam all die."[7]

Fox claims that the Old Testament never suggests such a doctrine and replaces it with what he feels to be the driving force agenda of the early stories of Genesis: creation-centered spirituality. He called his book on the subject *Original Blessing*. This focuses on the positive, not the negative, hope, not pessimism. In many ways though, what we have here is a half-full glass where one theological perspective is concentrating on the glass being half empty and the other

on the fact that it is half full. Fox needs to challenge those
from an original sin perspective about the errors that have
arisen from an over-emphasis on the fall of man, rather than
the creation of God. He has strong points of critique that
need to be heard. There has been a tendency to concentrate
on duty and discipline and ignore beauty, freedom, art, and
imagination. There is an over-emphasis on the righteousness
of the individual at the expense of justice for the entire world
and too much stress on the individual instead of community.
This mind-set can become very negative and damning and
lead to an ascetic dualistic view of life. However, an entirely
new paradigm might not be the answer to critique the more
traditional thinking.

In the end, every theological position will be misinterpreted
and misused, will push itself off balance and have errors that
humanity brings to any idea no matter how originally pure.
Fox's Creation Spirituality has the danger of very quickly
eradicating the mirror that sin is for us, to see a reflection
of our faulty condition. Our awareness and understanding
of our condition is a wonderful rein on the excesses that
we as human beings can too speedily languish in. An old
history teacher of mine taught us that the greatest men and
women of history were those who were acutely aware of their
weaknesses, and thus were able to take action to avoid their
consequences. So a knowledge of sin is like the boxer who,
knowing he has a cut eye, will not fight in such a free and easy
manner that the cut would open enough to cause his defeat.
Tom Waits is like the fan at the side of the ring screaming
articulate and literary descriptions of the goriness of the cut.

As a result of his concentration on things dark and sinful,
many have accused Waits of being godless. Even Ireland's
Hot Press magazine that is not in any way keen to find Jesus
in anything called *Blood Money* a "Jesusless" album. In that
same interview with Terry Gross on *Fresh Air*, she mentions
a song, "Down There By The Train," that Waits wrote for the

late Johnny Cash:

FRESH AIR INTERVIEWER: "It's funny, when the singer sings it, it sounds like an unusual spiritual, and usually you write about godlessness.

WAITS: Godlessness? Really? Oh!

FA: Wouldn't you say?

WAITS: I don't know about that.

FA: The absence of God.

TW: I don't know. Do you think so?

FA: Well some of the songs. Well one explicitly "God's Away On Business."

TW: Oh, okay. Well, he's away. He's not gone. He's just away. You have to understand He was on business. A guy like Him has got to be busy, looking after a lot of things.

It is impossible in words to actually describe the surprise and consternation in Waits' voice that his music should be labeled such. The impression is certainly that it has never crossed his mind. There are many little glimpses of grace and Jesus in Waits' work. It is not predominant by any means, and if you are not looking, as obviously Terri wasn't, then you could miss it, just like life really! But just like life, God is there to be found and to give another hue to the black underbelly of the human experience. That song, given to the late Johnny Cash for his fantastic American Recording series, oozes a confident hope in old time redemption where *you'll be washed of all your sins*. What will wash the sin? The blood of the lamb!

The Cash song is not just an isolated incident. The Blind Boys

Of Alabama with their sixty-year-old fermented brew of gospel and blues recast two of Waits' songs on their 2001 album, *Spirit Of The Century*. "Jesus Gonna Be Here Soon" is taken out of the scariest of all Waits albums, *Bone Machine*, and the despairing characters of Waits' population and is given a hopeful expectant celebratory gospel feel. There is still the confession of a drink habit that God knows about, and God seems to be aware that he is made of dust and allows for the frailty. "Way Down In The Hole" seems a likely location for all characters Waitsian, but it is the devil that we are trying to keep down here in a song that begins in the Garden, just as mankind did. Sadly, Waits' warning for humanity to watch its back comes just the entire length of human history too late.

The most epic mercy-drenched gospel song in Waits' career is when he guests on classical composer Gavin Bryars album *Jesus Blood Has Never Failed Me Yet*. Bryars had found a cassette tape of a tramp singing the traditional old hymn. It was ragged, frail, and you could almost feel the freezing cold of the street and touch the texture of the cardboard shelter and the newspaper blanket. Very Waits! Just as vivid is the truth of the words of the hymn. Here is a man with nothing finding transcendent hope and comfort. There is no quick-fix solution. He is not looking for one. Spiritual reality for the tramp is not some miraculous turn around of circumstances that would lead him into a comfortable semi-detached house on the stockbroker belt of London where he would find himself leading an Alpha group in a lively Church Of England fellowship and a member of the golf club. Those things had nothing to do with the deal that God gives. This tramp has never known the blood of Christ to fail him. It finds him where he is and sustains him in his lack of material sustenance.

That Tom Waits should get involved in such a project is perfect. The depth of emotion that this ad lib song caused led Bryars to compose a piece of music around it. Tom Waits added his voice to that of the tramp. These are the people

169 | THIRTEEN

he loves. These are the people to whom he brings dignity. In spite of the wretchedness of a world where you could easily believe "God's Away on Business," there is belief, and that belief changes things. Here on the street, his most beloved habitat, Waits gets to sing a duet in a near intimate fellowship with a fellow soul who wants to sing praise.

If it is Tom Waits singing praise you want, then those Blind Boys Of Alabama have brought it into being. In late 2003 The Blind Boys released their Christmas album *Go Tell It On The Mountain*, and who should they get to sing on the title track? That voice that is like sin and the Old Testament and frogs and snails and puppy dogs tails sings about the good news of Christ's Gospel with an authority that needs the grit in the vocal but also the reality in the living. Sin and salvation go together and never more perfectly than when Tom Waits sings about both! Godless? Tom Waits? No way!

NOTES

INTRODUCTION
1. Steve Stockman, *Caress of God's Grace (Am I Looking)*, New Home/Fresh Beginning (Badger Books, Belfast, 2004).

LOOKING FOR THE TRUTH WHERE IT SHOULDN'T BELONG
1. Patrick Kavanagh, *Street Corner Christ, The Complete Poems* (The Goldsmith Press, Ireland, 1975).
2. John Stott, *The Contemporary Christian* (IVP, Leicester, England, 1992), p. 27.
3. Ibid.
4. Ibid., p. 28.
5. John Stott, *The Incomparable Christ* (IVP, Leicester, England, 2001).
6. Acts 17:16-34 (NIV, International Bible Society, 1978).
7. 1 Corinthians 9:16 (NIV, International Bible Society, 1978).
8. Luke 10:27 (NIV, International Bible Society, 1978).

BOB DYLAN
1. Ian McDonald, *No Direction Home, Uncut* (London), June 2002.
2. Jim Sclavunos, *No Direction Home, Uncut* (London), June 2002.
3. Greil Marcus, *Invisible Republic* (Picador, London, 1997), p. ix.
4. Bob Geldof, *No Direction Home, Uncut* (London), June 2002.
5. Greil Marcus, *Invisible Republic* (Picador, London, 1997), p. 22.
6. Anthony Scaduto, *Bob Dylan* (Abacus, London, 1972), p. 153.
7. Woody Guthrie, *Bound For Glory* (Plume, London, 1943), p. 19.
8. Linda Solomon, *Village Voice* as quoted by David Hajdu, *Positively 4th Street* (Bloomsbury, London, 2002), p. 163.

9. Andy Gill, *My Back Pages* (Carlton Books, London, 1998), p. 28.
10. David Magee, *An Analysis Of the Roots Of Martin Luther's Philosophy of Non Violence* (M.Phil Queens University Belfast, 2001).
11. David Magee, *An Analysis Of the Roots Of Martin Luther's Philosophy of Non Violence* (M.Phil Queens University Belfast, 2001) quoting Martin Luther King, *Why We Can't Wait* (Mentor, USA, 1963).
12. Amos 5:21-24 (NIV, International Bible Society, 1978).
13. Martin Luther King Jr., *A Knock At Midnight*, ed. Clayborne Carson (Warner Books, USA, 1998), as quoted by David Magee, *An Analysis Of the Roots Of Martin Luther's Philosophy of Non Violence* (M.Phil Queens University Belfast, 2001).
14. Andy Gill, *My Back Pages* (Carlton Books, London, 1998), p. 44.
15. Clinton Heylin, *Behind The Shades* (Viking, England, 2000), p. 126.
16. Matthew 20:16 (NIV Bible, International Bible Society, 1978).
18. Martin Luther King Jr. letter from Birmingham Jail as edited by Clayborne Carson, *The Autobiography of Martin Luther* (Abacus Books, London, 1999), p. 199-200.
19. Andy Gill, *My Back Pages* (Carlton Books, London, 1998), p. 37.

20. Frances Taylor, "Dylan disowns his protest songs," edited Craig McGregor, *Bob Dylan: A Retrospective* (Picador, London, 1972) p.72.
21. Joan Baez, *And A Voice To Sing With* (Arrow Books, London, 1988).
22. Joe Klein, *Woody Guthrie: A Life* (Alfred A Knopf. Inc., USA, 1980), p.430.
23. Paul Williams, *Bob Dylan Performing Artist 1960-73* (Xanadu Books, 1990), p. 149-150.
24. Dylan to Nat Hentoff as quoted by Paul Williams, *Bob Dylan Performing Artist 1960-73* (Xanadu Books, 1990) p. 149-150.

KURT COBAIN

1. Ecclesiastes 1:2 (NIV, International Bible Society, 1978).
2. Ecclesiastes 1:8 (NIV, International Bible Society, 1978).
3. Doug Coupland, *Life After God* (Simon and Schuster, London, 1994), p. 177-178.
4. Phil Sutcliffe, *King Of Pain*, Q, December 1993.
5. Michael Azerrad, *Come As You Are* (Virgin Books, 1993), p. 17.
6. Jon Savage, "Sounds Dirty: The Truth About Nirvana," *The Observer* (London), August 13, 1993.
7. Kurt Cobain, *Journals*, (Penguin, London, 2002), p.269.
8. Ian Tilton, "The 100 Greatest Rock N Roll Photographs," Q, p. 193.
9. Charles R. Cross interviewed by Internet Nirvana Fan Club, 2001, *http://www.nirvanaclub.com.*
10. Charles R. Cross, *Heavier Than Heaven* (Sceptre, London, 2001), p. ix.
11. Genesis 3:6.
12. Charles R. Cross, "The Man Behind The Mask," Q, October 2002.
13. Christopher Sandford, *Kurt Cobain*, (Orion, London, 2001), p. 17.
14. Ecclesiastes 1:11 (NIV, International Bible Society, 1978).
15. Douglas Coupland, *Life After God* (Simon and Schuster, London, 1994), p. 359.
16. 2 Corinthians 4:17 (NIV, International Bible Society, 1978).
17. Matthew 6:19-20 (NIV, International Bible Society, 1978).
18. Luke 12:19 (NIV, International Bible Society, 1978).
19. Hebrews 4:15 (NIV, International Bible Society, 1978).

GEORGE HARRISON

1. Bob Geldof, *The Guardian* (London), December 1, 2001.
2. George Harrison, Press Conference, 1974.
3. Olivia Harrison, *Harrison* by the editors of *Rolling Stone* (Simon and Schuster Inc., USA, 2002), p. 8-9.
4. Ibid.
5. George Harrison as quoted by Olivia Harrison, *Harrison* by the editors of *Rolling Stone* (Simon and Schuster Inc., USA, 2002), p. 8-9.
6. George Harrison interviewed by Mukunda Goswami, *Hare Krishna*

Mantra—There's Nothing Higher, 1982, http://ww.krishna.org.

7. George Harrison, *I Me Mine* (Simon and Schuster, New York, 1980), p. 200.

8. Ibid., p. 258.

9. Ephesians 2:8-9 (NIV, International Bible Society, 1978).

10. George Harrison interviewed by Mukunda Goswami, *Hare Krishna Mantra—There's Nothing Higher*, 1982, http://www.krishna.org.

11. George Harrison interviewed by Mukunda Goswami, *Hare Krishna Mantra—There's Nothing Higher*, 1982, http://www.krishna.org.

12. George Harrison, *I Me Mine* (Simon and Schuster, New York, 1980), p. 180-181.

RADIOHEAD

1. *Shawshank Redemption* (Castle Rock Entertainment).

2. Luke 8:1-15.

3. Thom Yorke in interview with John Robinson, "It's Clear And Pretty But I Think People Won't Get It," *NME*, May 3, 2003.

4. Ibid.

5. Rosemary Cowan, *Cornel West: The Politics Of Redemption* (Polity, UK, 2003), p. 25.

6. Ibid.

7. Thom Yorke interviewed by Phil Sutcliffe, "Death Is All Around," *Q*, October 1997.

8. 2 Corinthians 4:18 (NIV, International Bible Society, 1978).

9. Os Guiness, *Gravedigger File* (Hodder and Stoughton, London, 1984), p. 16.

10. *The Truman Show* (Paramount Pictures, 1998).

11. Steve Stockman, Rhythms Of Redemption, *http://stocki.ni.org*.

12. David Fricke, "Bitter Prophet," *Rolling Stone*, June 26, 2003.

13. Thom Yorke interviewed by Michael Odell, "Silence Genius At Work," *Q*, July 2003.

14. Ibid.

15. David Fricke, "Bitter Prophet," *Rolling Stone*, June 26, 2003.

16. David Dark, *Everyday Apocalypse* (Brazos Press, USA, 2002), p. 67.

JONI MITCHELL

1. *Goldmine*, February 17, 1995 as quoted by Karen O'Brien, *Shadows And Light* (Virgin Books, London, 2001), p. 101.

2. Stephen Holden, *New York Times*, March 17, 1991 as featured in *The Joni Mitchell Companion*, ed. Stacy Luftig (Shirmer Books, New York, 2000).

3. Phil Sutcliffe, *Q* magazine, 1988, as featured in *The Joni Mitchell Companion*, ed. Stacy Luftig (Shirmer Books, New York, 2000).

4. Iain Blair, *Los Angeles Herald*, March 9, 1986 as featured in *The Joni Mitchell Companion*, ed. Stacy Luftig (Shirmer Books, New York, 2000).

5. Karen O'Brien, *Shadows And Light* (Virgin Books, London, 2001), p. 214.

6. Barney Hoskins, *Mojo* (London), December 1994.

7. Joni Mitchell, in the liner notes to *The Complete Geffen Recordings* (Geffen Records, 2003).

JACKSON BROWNE

1. Rich Wiseman, *The Story of a Hold Out* (USA, 1980).

2. Acts 4:32-35 (NIV, International Bible Society, 1978).

DAVID GRAY

1. Photograph by Ben Curtis as in *The Independent on Sunday* (London), July 13, 2003.

2. David Gray in an interview with Colin Harper in 1994 as quoted by Michael Heatley, *David Gray; A Biography* (Omnibus Press, London, 2000).

3. Interview with Kim Porcelli, "David Verses The Goliath," *Hot Press* (Dublin), July 2003.

4. Bono to Aengus Fanning, "Bono Vox," *Sunday Independent* (Dublin), June 29, 2003.

5. Matthew 5:13.
6. Matthew 5:14-16.

BRUCE SPRINGSTEEN

1. Dave Marsh, *Glory Days* (Pantheon Books, USA, 1987), p. 344.
2. Bruce Springsteen on "New York Serenade" from the *Live In New York City* DVD (Columbia, 2001).
3. James Henke, "Bruce Springsteen: The Rolling Stone Interview," *Rolling Stone*, August 6, 1992.
4. Ibid.
5. Bill Flanagan, *Written In My Soul* (Omnibus, USA, 1986-87), p. 142.
6. Bruce Springsteen, *Songs* (Avon Books Inc., USA, 1998), p. 136.
7. Ibid., p. 139.
8. Acts 5:12-21 (NIV, International Bible Society, 1978).
9. Bruce Springsteen, *Songs* (Avon Books Inc., USA, 1998), p. 217.
10. James Henke, "Bruce Springsteen: The Rolling Stone Interview," *Rolling Stone*, August 6, 1992.
11. Ibid.
12. Ibid.
13. Bruce Springsteen, *Songs* (Avon Books Inc., USA, 1998), p. 276-277.

ANI DIFRANCO

1. Ani DiFranco interviewed by Lydia Hutchinson, "The Little Folk Singer Who Could," *Performing Songwriter*, June 1999.
2. Steve Stockman, *September 11th Prayer, New Home/Fresh Beginning* (Badger Books, Belfast, 2004).
3. Luke 9:24-25.

BOB MARLEY

1. Cedella Booker, *Bob Marley: An Intimate Portrait By His Mother* (Penguin, London, 1997), p. 147.
2. Ian Boyne, *Jamaica: Breaking Barriers between Churches and Rastafarians*, 1983, as quoted by William David Spencer, *Dread Jesus* (SPCK, London, 1999), p. 166.
3. Ibid., p. 167.
4. James 2:20 (NIV, International Bible Society, 1978).

LAURYN HILL

1. Romans 5:17 (NIV, International Bible Society, 1978).
2. Ibid.
3. John 14:27.
4. John 19:30.

TOM WAITS

1. Matthew 9:12 (NIV, International Bible Society, 1978).
2. Mark 19:30 (NIV, International Bible Society, 1978).
3. Cath Carroll, *Tom Waits* (Unanimous Ltd., London, 2000), p. 1.
4. Jeremiah 17:9 (NIV, International Bible Society, 1978).
5. Romans 5:12 (NIV, International Bible Society, 1978).
6. Romans 5:17 (NIV, International Bible Society, 1978).
7. 1 Corinthians 15:22 (NIV, International Bible Society, 1978).

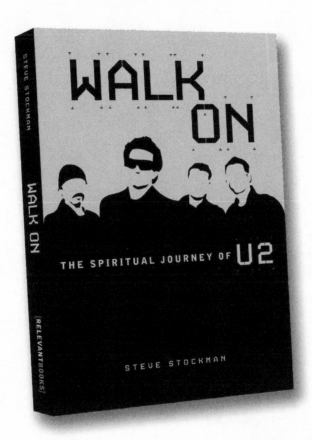

Get a FREE ISSUE of
RELEVANT magazine!
God. life. progressive culture.